CONGRATULATIONS – YOU'RE A SENIOR CITIZEN

A LIGHT- HEARTED GUIDE TO HELP ANYONE
WHO HAS REACHED THE TRUE AGE OF
MATURITY TO FULFIL THEIR POTENTIAL
AS A SENIOR CITIZEN

BARRY HILL

Published in 2007 by Sommhill Books,
Cheadle Hulme. Cheshire. SK8 7JR
sommhillbooks@btinternet.com

A catalogue record for this book is available from the British
Library.

ISBN -13 978-0-9555384-0-7

Printed and bound in Great Britain

CONTENTS

FOREWORD

Forget the flirty thirties, the naughty forties, the thrifty fifties. As far as you are concerned, they are history.

Congratulations! You are now a Senior Citizen. It's official, as your birth certificate will testify.

But there is more - much more - to being a Senior Citizen than reaching a certain landmark in age terms. You are about to take on a role that your entire previous existence has been preparing you for - that of elder statesman, mentor, guru, guide and leader. Guardian of the good, doyen of decency and purveyor of perfection.

Assuming the mantle of Senior Citizen is no undertaking to be approached lightly. You have inherited a fine tradition. You have reached the age of maturity, been elevated to that highly-exalted position from whence you are set to fulfil your destiny. To preserve all things that are worth preserving – everything that you stand for - while relentlessly fighting all things that are evil - all those things of which you disapprove.

You have a duty to lead your fellow travellers along life's pitfall-strewn highway by example, particularly those younger and less experienced than yourself. To educate them in the intricate weave of life's rich tapestry.

By strange coincidence, you will find that this includes just about everyone who doesn't share your views. As you get older, you may wish to amend this to just about everyone.

For some, this responsibility sits happily on their shoulders. Much of the content of this practical guide will come as second nature. But for those not so blessed with such natural ability, being a good and effective Senior Citizen may not come so easily. It has to be worked at.

The Senior Citizen is entitled to speak with authority on practically anything under the sun. Because whatever the subject, your generation invented it, developed it, or refined it, as any Senior Citizen will tell you at every opportunity.

By reaching the golden milestone of Senior Citizenship, you will have acquired many characteristics that are typical of your generation, characteristics that are unfortunately sadly lacking in others - wisdom, serenity, selflessness, fair-mindedness.

Never deny these qualities. Wear them with pride, for without these basic qualities of life, civilisation has no future.

Education, sophistication, taste, manners, character, moral fibre, standards – above all, standards - physical and mental well-being, dress sense, a strong sense of responsibility and a deep appreciation of the true values of life.

Today's Senior Citizen is of an era when not only did all these qualities matter, they were part and parcel of our every-day existence. Sadly, they are rapidly disappearing in the so-called culture of the New Millennium.

So it is the duty of everyone who aspires to the role of Senior Citizen to halt this downward slide of civilisation, to turn back the tide of revolting revolution and to show that there is only one way forward for mankind – the right way.

Our way.

The aim of this guide is to help everyone who has reached the age of maturity to fulfil their true potential as a Senior Citizen. To be able to hold their heads up high as they battle to maintain the standards and traditions inherited from their forbears and so painstakingly guarded during their lifetime.

The standards of the Senior Citizen are the only standards. It is the duty of every Senior Citizen to lead by example.

Within these pages, fellow missionaries, is your very own ABC of Senior Citizenship. Learn it well. Go forth and spread the word. There is only one way. One truth. One light.

The gospel according to the Senior Citizen.

ADVICE

Perhaps the most effective way Senior Citizens can make their presence felt is through the advice they are so selflessly and readily prepared to give to others, whether they want it or not.

It can be applied to most situations, comes as second nature to the majority and costs absolutely nothing.

'We never did it like that in our day' is a good opening line, but perhaps not quite so good as 'I can see you've never done this before'.

The best opportunities for giving advice usually stem from close to home, in fact one's own family. They have no idea how to run a home, bring up children, conduct their lives. But more about that when we come to deal with families.

It is by no means, however, only family members who have exclusive rights to the benefit of your experience.

Every day, opportunities arise for you to freely give advice to all manner of folk. The fact that much of it will be unwelcome and the rest totally ignored should not in any way deter you from continuing to give it. Any intransigent attitude by the recipient of such advice is certainly no reflection on you, but merely serves to underline the insular attitude of anyone who has not yet reached the status of Senior Citizen.

Tradesmen provide ideal opportunities for the giving of advice.

For example, should you have cause to call in a plumber or electrician, you should make it abundantly clear from the outset that you have summoned his assistance not because you are incapable of doing the job yourself, but simply because you do not have the time.

You then go on to talk him through whatever job he is doing stage by stage, and if the eventual outcome is a trip to Accident and Emergency Department to have a monkey wrench removed from a certain part of one's anatomy, it is a small price to pay for ensuring that the tradesman goes away not only considerably richer, but much better versed in his craft – thanks to your advice.

There are basically two types of advice where you can make your presence felt – advice that isn't solicited, and advice that is. Unsolicited advice should be offered wherever and whenever an opportunity arises, even though it may not always be appreciated to the full. Solicited advice is a totally different beast, and one to be relished by any Senior Citizen fortunate enough to come across it.

Always remember, when you have attained Senior Citizen status, you are expected to know everything. So don't disappoint those less fortunate than yourself. Never admit you don't know.

If someone asks you a question, you can be absolutely sure of one thing –they don't know the answer, or they wouldn't be asking you. So within reason you can tell them anything.

Seeking directions is a common way for your assistance to be sought. 'Could you tell me the best way to…' is truly a question that should gladden the heart of any Senior Citizen.

By the time the inquirer has found out that the information you gave was based more on imagination than fact, and they have ended up back where they started – which will be inevitable - you will be long gone.

So give advice freely whether it is sought or not, offer it at every opportunity and always speak with confidence and conviction. Never express any self- doubt. This can only serve to undermine your authority and cast doubt over any claim on your part to be the font of all wisdom and knowledge.

APPEARANCE

Basically, Senior Citizens come in two varieties - male and female. In many cases, it is not that easy to tell the difference.

Perhaps the most sure-fire giveaway is the hair. If there isn't a total lack of it, it is more often than not in all the wrong places.

In the male of the species, this generally means growing out of the nose, out of the ears and just about every other orifice, but little or none growing out of the scalp; while in the case of the female, a generous covering on the arms, legs and upper lip is often a strong pointer to the lady in question having reached Senior Citizen status.

When the youth of today - male or female - sport heads smoother than a billiard ball, their lack of cranial thatch intended to indicate that they are truly children of the new Millennium, they are a good generation or two behind the times. Senior Citizens have already been there. Seen it. Done it. Bought the tee shirt. There was only one style when you were youngsters – short back and sides, and do I mean short!

They may think that by sporting hair in any colour of the rainbow, it makes them different. Who do they think they're kidding?

Anyone who had their head swamped in gentian violet as a kid to guard against any one of a number of infections, many of them a total figment of a doting mother's imagination, knew what it felt like to be walking round like a fruit lollipop 50 years ago.

And when it comes to dress, the youngsters of today with their sloppy, ill-fitting, torn clothes that were obviously made for someone several sizes larger; tatty trainers without laces; and ill-fitting headgear may consider themselves style-conscious leaders of fashion.

Frequently they sport so-called 'designer' stubble indicative of someone who has been forced to spend the last few weeks of their dreary life in a very dark cave.

Well have we got news for them.

That was the fashion more than fifty years ago, when kids were dressed in whatever their elder brothers and sisters had grown out of. When a shoe with a lace was a luxury and a razor blade with anything like a decent cutting edge was something to be treasured.

The clothes of your generation were selected for their practicality, not out of an urge to line the pockets of the fashion gurus. For every child who grew out of something, there was another ready to grow into it. Heaven help any poor lad who had an elder sister. He was likely to be turned out in cotton dress and frilly knickers for the entire duration of his school life.

First up, best dressed was the rule – no danger.

But you evolved. Not like today's youngsters, who seem to be going back by leaps and bounds to the stone age.

You have grown in stature and sophistication all through your lives. And undoubtedly it shows.

You should be instantly recognised today at first glance for the Senior Citizens you are by your impeccable dress sense.

The string vest and liberty bodice may find little favour among the young of today, with their bare midriffs and nether regions barely covered by some ragged strip of material that looks as if its been used to clean paint brushes. But they were items of clothing that had a definite purpose in life. They formed the basis on which to build a sensible dress code which has stood the test of time, spanned the generations and is still followed with pride by any self-respecting Senior Citizen to this very day.

When it comes to fashion statements, be proud. Show the world that what you are is what you wear – solid, dependable, durable. Never forget that appearance is all-important. You never get a second chance to make a first impression.

The male Senior Citizen should always strive to appear in public dressed in jacket and tie, whatever the weather and whatever the activity in which he is taking part. If he can remember the optional colour co-ordinated handkerchief, neatly-folded and peeping out of his top pocket, so much the better.

For the ladies, a matching twin set with colour co-ordinated trousers – or indeed a trouser suit – should be the fashion statement to the outside world.

At one time, it would have been unthinkable for a lady to appear in public in trousers, and there is one small-minded ignorant section of society who erroneously believe that they are worn by the more mature woman to hide the varicose veins and cellulite. Nothing could be further from the truth, as we well know. Ample trousers on a mature woman say freedom of movement, action woman, eternal youth.

If you are a male Senior Citizen, and you walk along the street during the hottest August on record, dressed in white cap, regimental blazer, colour matching shirt and tie and Oxford brogues, or if you are a female Senior Citizen in your tweed suit cut as severe as the expression on your face, you can be absolutely sure that you will not fail to attract the notice of the younger generation.

And they will get the message loud and clear that by your display of unique dress sense you are undoubtedly a fine upstanding example of a bygone age who stands for so much that is sadly lacking in this modern world.

They may not actually put these sentiments into those exact words, but they will certainly not fail to note the full message of your statement.

When it comes to fashion, Senior Citizens are in a class of their own.

BAD HABITS

Bad habits are what other people have – never yourselves.

Many Senior Citizens wear spectacles. And it is often a constant source of irritation to younger members of the family in particular that said spectacles are so often allowed to lead a life of their own.

If Senior Citizens were to add up the total number of hours in any twelve months spent looking for mis-placed spectacles – for most of the time, they are wearing them anyway – they would probably find that they had lost at least a fortnight of their lives. At least that would be the view of anyone who didn't understand the Senior Citizen.

Not every Senior Citizen, however, wears spectacles to alleviate failing eyesight. Oh no. Many of us wear them as a fashion accessory, to enhance our appearance, give an impression of wisdom, sophistication, character and charm - in fact everything a Senior Citizen stands for.

And what better way of drawing attention to yourself and your undoubted qualities than feigning to misplace the one obvious item that sums up everything you stand for – your spectacles! So what may appear to be a bad habit by those who fail to understand and appreciate the ploy, to Senior Citizens it is a cunning way of focussing attention on themselves, thus providing yet another opportunity to make themselves the centre of attention.

Many Senior Citizens find themselves asking for everything that is said to them to be repeated. This could also be construed in some quarters as a bad habit, particularly by the young and ignorant.

Nothing could be further from the truth.

When Senior Citizens persistently come out with 'What was that again, dearie?' it is because they wish to confirm the subject matter of the inquiry in order to give a considered response.

Unfortunately, today. so many folk – not Senior Citizens, I hasten to add – are so wrapped up in themselves and their own little worlds that they haven't time to listen properly to the woes and cares of others. You must make it clear that your request for a question to be repeated is merely emphasising that you are giving the inquirer your undivided attention.

Asking the same question over and over again is another example of how you may give the erroneous impression that you have picked up another bad habit along the road to senility. Utter nonsense.

If any Senior Citizen asks the same question repeatedly, it is again out of nothing but consideration for others. By frequently repeating the question, you are not only ensuring that the question is fully understood, but also giving the other person the opportunity to change the answer, should they so wish.

Talking too loudly about other people while in their earshot; pointing at strangers and remarking on some aspect of their behaviour or appearance in tones that can be heard at least two blocks away are also regarded by many younger folk as so-called bad habits acquired by the Senior Citizen.

What utter nonsense. If there is one thing that you have learned over a lifetime's experience, it is that honesty is the best policy and if you have a genuine comment to make about anything or anyone, it is best that the object of that comment is well aware of your feelings. Where is the point in uttering the thought in the first place if no one is aware of it? Never mind the consequences. Fearless to a fault, that is the motto of the Senior Citizen.

Other habits which are disgusting in others but perfectly acceptable when performed in public by the Senior Citizen are laughing loudly at your own jokes; scratching yourself anywhere below the waist; and taking your teeth out in other people's company.

Don't feel too guilty if I have mentioned a habit here that you have not yet indulged in yourself. I can assure you that, given time, you will!

BON VIVEUR

No one knows more about good living than the Senior Citizen. We should do. It is another thing that we invented.

No one can speak on the subject of good living - even attempt to define it, let alone understand it – unless they have experienced life at the other end of the scale.

As you well know, after the war living well was having a smidgeon of fat to spread on your bread; enough sweet coupons left over for two ounces of bulls eyes at weekends to keep the kids happy; and meat on the table once a fortnight. Harsh days indeed.

But we always had the potential for enjoying life to the full because we were brought up to make the best of what life had to offer. What we lacked in material things, we more than made up for in resilience and the ability to overcome adversity.

And only by emphasising these facts to the younger generation at every conceivable opportunity can you be sure that the traditions so painstakingly carved in history by yourselves will survive well into the 21st Century - or at least until you are out of earshot.

You may not have had two halfpennies to rub together, but that didn't stop you enjoying the good life.

No saunas, power showers and jacuzzis for you before popping down to the bar and grill. Height of luxury in the personal hygiene department was a bath in the tin tub in front of the fire on a Friday night. If you were really lucky, there may be a dripping dipper for supper.

But that didn't stop you enjoying yourselves. Poor you may have been, but you had standards. You'd never be caught in a dirty vest. Because you had pride.

You may not have had televisions, washing machines, and fridge freezers. You used to work a 12 hour day, six days a week, and the reason you used to enjoy your leisure time, such as it was, was because it was well earned.

Every penny you took home, everything you owned in the world had to be sweated over, so when that pay packet appeared on a Friday night and next day a carpet sweeper made its grand entrance into a household – even though it was bought second hand – there was a pride behind it all that no one could put a value on.

Life was undoubtedly a struggle, but one borne with pride. You knew how to make the most of what you had. It was all about not what you had, but what you made of it.

And that's the message you have to get through to the younger generation today. At every opportunity.

'Things were never like that in our day.' Is always a good opening line before going on to regale the listener with every relevant detail – and some not so relevant - of what things <u>were</u> like in our day. 'But we knew how to enjoy ourselves' is always a good closing line. What can anyone say to follow that?

You'll probably find at this stage that your listener will make a hurried getaway. Because they will have realised that there is no point arguing with a Senior Citizen who most certainly knows the meaning of enjoying life to the full, whatever their personal circumstances.

Next time you are in the presence of someone who is draped in designer clothing, enjoys five star meals in the most exotic eating-out spots, and whose conversation is littered with references to vintage wines, just ask yourself if they get as much enjoyment out of their lifestyle as you got out of draining the last dregs from a discarded bottle of brown ale nicked from the yard at the back of the off licence as you walked home in your ill-fitting shoes with three pennorth of chips and a bag of scratchings.

When you come across a fellow traveller, living life in the fast lane of life's highway, who has just come back from some exotic location, travelling first class, using his mobile phone to keep in touch with his banker and stockbroker, and who has managed to make another £10m at the stroke of a pen while he's been away, ask yourself 'Is he happy?' 'Is he truly happy?'

Bon viveur? They don't know the meaning of the word.

CHARACTER

You have spent the past 60-plus years building your character, because you have had to find your own way in life. You have got where you are today through sheer grit and determination, battling overwhelming odds, overcoming seemingly insurmountable obstacles – something that today's younger generation have never had to endure because they have never had to put up with what we had to put up with through those formative years of our youth and on into the big, wide world.

Your life – and your character – has always been built on a secure, solid base. On a belt and braces approach to everything you do. Nothing is left to chance.

Many Senior Citizens constantly demonstrate this fact by checking that all the doors and windows are locked at night , all the lights are turned off, not just once, but many times. To the casual observer, appearing to be unable to remember what you did three minutes ago may be misconstrued as a sure sign of the onset of senility. But to the Senior Citizen it is just one more way of reinforcing the strength of character that you have spent a lifetime acquiring.

It started in your school days, of course, where you very quickly learned the meaning of discipline. Work hard, play hard – that was what your lives were all about. And it didn't do a single one of you any harm at all. It taught you lessons that have stood you in good stead all your life as you have struggled against all odds to get where you are today. And to lay the foundations for generations to come.

So whenever you come across a student who is about to leave University with a £25,000 loan to repay; no prospect of ever owning so much as a garden shed of their own; knowing that it could take months to find a job if they're lucky, make it very clear to them that if it hadn't been for your sacrifices in the past, they wouldn't have had such a firm foundation on which to build their future.

You may find that occasionally you come up against someone who does not exactly share your rose-tinted view of their situation. In this case you have two options.

You can walk away, because you know they don't have your patience, command of the English language or degree of understanding to become involved in a constructive discussion on the subject.

Or you can point out to them that you never lived on state handouts, played computer games from breakfast to bedtime and stayed at so-called colleges until the onset of middle age. You rolled up your sleeves and got on with the important things in life – earning a living and building for a sound future.

This latter approach is a real indication of your character, and could well have far-reaching consequences by changing the course of their lives – or, more likely, yours.

CHIVALRY

Chivalry is a word that doesn't exist in the vocabulary of the youth of today.

Chivalry is much more than common courtesy. It embodies courage, honour justice and a ready willingness to help those less fortunate than oneself.

Wear these qualities with pride. Don't allow the old standards and traditions to be swallowed up in a sea of selfishness.

If you see a short-sighted fellow being by the side of a busy road, take their arm and see them safely across. Your selfless act will attract instant gratitude and show any onlooker that you really care and are not afraid to show it.

This approach could, occasionally, throw up a slight problem if the said fellow being didn't want to cross the road in the first place and mistook you for a serial mugger. If this should happen, you indicate that you do not speak or understand English, and you leave the scene as fast as possible, preferably before the arrival of the police.

Courage in the face of adversity and a strong sense of justice are other hallmarks of the Senior Citizen. Here again you must be prepared to demonstrate, often under the most difficult circumstances, that you are never afraid to face up to your responsibilities as a defender or all things right.

If you should come across a young couple in the street obviously airing a difference of opinion, approach them in a confident but friendly way.

Announce in clear tones 'I am a Senior Citizen and as such am more than qualified in experience and wisdom to mediate in this dispute.'

The two adversaries will more than likely be so surprised at your chivalry and concern for their welfare that they will forget their original dispute and immediately find a new spirit of alliance, channelling their anger from each other – to you. At this point, you will make a hasty departure if you wish to see your next birthday, but you will have set a fine example in the meaning of true courage as well as demonstrating that the age of chivalry is definitely not dead..

As for honour, it goes without saying that all Senior Citizens were at the front of the queue when this attribute was dealt out. Guardians of all that is right and proper, held in the highest respect by all. What better description could there be of the Senior Citizen?

Next time you see a belligerent teenager with 'HATE' tattooed across his forehead and a safety pin through his nose with his feet up on the seat of the bus, you could calmly and politely point out to him the error of his ways.

'Young man, you really shouldn't have your boots up on that seat,' is a good opening line. It gets right to the heart of the problem. It focuses the attention of the miscreant on your good self, and encompasses the entire problem in one brief sentence. Should you feel the need to qualify your comment, you could always add: 'Folk have got to sit there'.

I doubt whether he will actually say 'You are a Senior Citizen and I hold you in the highest respect', but I would be very surprised if your remarks went unnoticed.

He will probably be so grateful to you for pointing out the error of his ways, so admiring of your sense of responsibility towards others that he will almost certainly make at least one suggestion as to an alternative resting place for his boots. At this point, it may be advisable to have put some distance between yourself and the young offender – preferably at least a couple of bus stops.

I am sure you will by now have the point, dear reader. Courage, honour and justice spell chivalry. Appreciation of your efforts to spread the word may not immediately be apparent, but as you lie in a hospital bed, reflecting on the events of the past 24 hours that led to you being there, you will be overcome by a deep sense of satisfaction, happy in the knowledge that you have made a positive impact on someone's life – even if it is only your own.

COMPETITIONS

Any Senior Citizen will tell you that the key to eternal youth is to keep body and mind active. We will come to the activities of the body under a different heading, but here we are concerned purely with the mind.

Competitions undoubtedly play a large part in the waking hours of Senior Citizens, and many onlookers consider it is just a way of passing the time.

Nothing could be further from the truth. Competitions – particularly crosswords – play an important part in maintaining the sharpness of mind, and increasing the vast general knowledge, the fine tuning and acute reasoning powers of the Senior Citizen.

So you owe it to yourself to get stuck into a crossword puzzle at every opportunity. Incidentally, if you really want to impress friends and relatives who may wish to know if you would like anything special for your birthday or Christmas, ask them for a book of crosswords, the more difficult the better. You're not going to do them anyway, but the person who buys them for you doesn't know that. The object of the exercise is to demonstrate your higher level of intellect.

If you haven't yet reached the dizzy heights of successfully completing your own personal crossword puzzle book - and be warned, a tremendous amount of self discipline is needed because the answers will be at the back of the book - the daily newspaper provides a suitable and varied challenge, depending on which paper you take.

The only drawback here is that you will have to wait until the following day to find out that one elusive word that you need to complete the puzzle, but this is also a useful exercise in itself as it helps to develop patience, a quality that some folk feel diminishes in Senior Citizens in direct proportion to the advancement of years. This notion is nonsense, of course, and another example of the ignorance of the young when it comes to understanding those more mature than themselves.

It is probably advisable to start with the quick coffee time crossword, which initially may take you a fortnight to complete, before moving onto some of the more serious newspapers. But do be aware that completing your crossword in solitude gives but a speck of the satisfaction you will get out of doing it in the company of others. If you can add facial expressions and the odd sound effect, you will attract more attention to yourself and thus gain more satisfaction from completing the puzzle.

If you can find yourself a seat next to someone who is doing the same puzzle, it is an added bonus, and if the person happens to be considerably younger than you, it is a heaven-sent opportunity for you to totally assert your status.

Remember, the aim of this exercise is not to gain any enjoyment from doing the crossword puzzle. You can do that anytime on your own. The aim here is to appear to complete the puzzle – the more difficult, the better – faster than the other person, thus striking a telling blow for Senior Citizens everywhere by establishing once again your superiority not only in general knowledge, but in culture, scholarship and intellect.

So you take up your position in clear view of your target – the other puzzler – and after a quick glance at your paper, you then complete your puzzle as quickly as possible. You don't necessarily have to put in the right words – just so long as you appear to be doing so. Then when you have finished, give a little smile of satisfaction.

Anyone who has witnessed the lightning completion of your task will be looking at you in sheer amazement. Your fellow puzzler will have an expression of sheer disbelief. As you get up to leave, casually drop the paper on your vacated seat. Then turn to walk away. I can guarantee that your fellow puzzler will be halfway to your paper before you have taken your first step.

This is the point at which you have second thoughts, turn back, pick up the paper and walk away. You will thus leave the scene not only having established your intellectual superiority, but as the centre of attention and in complete control, which is what any Senior Citizen worthy of the name should always strive to achieve.

There are of course competitions other than crossword puzzles, and you can win some very useful prizes. One tip for the Senior Citizen: don't talk enthusiastically about them to anyone. Always ridicule such competitions and the people who do them. That way you won't be encouraging hordes of folk to also do them, thus cutting down your chances of winning.

Local radio is an excellent way of broadcasting the case for the Senior Citizen. There is nothing like a phone-in when it comes to making a name for yourself. Almost non-stop throughout the day, presenters are always running some competition or other . The more air time they can fill with chat, the easier their job.

So at every opportunity, Senior Citizens should get themselves on the radio, demonstrate their vast knowledge and wisdom to the masses, but above all, while they have the freedom of the airwaves, take the opportunity to impose their views and standards on a wider audience.

And never be afraid of finding yourself in the embarrassing position of not knowing an answer, or being humbled by an opponent. Radio is notorious for technical problems, so if you find yourself backed into a corner, all you have to do is hang up and blame it on somebody else.

DRIVING

Perhaps the greatest contribution the Senior Citizen can make to a safer world is on the road.

As each new generation is introduced to the motor car, so aggression has risen. This has been caused, in the main, by three factors - cars are increasing in performance all the time, presenting the constant challenge of using them to their capacity; the roads are becoming more crowded, leading to increased frustration; and most importantly, anyone younger than ourselves shows absolutely no consideration to other road users. So it is up to you once again to lead by example.

Just as pride in your personal appearance is important, so pride in the appearance of your chosen form of transport is equally paramount.

So every Sunday morning. it is essential that the vehicle be thoroughly cleaned inside and out, whether it needs it or not. It must be understood that a car cannot be over-cleaned.

Interior decorations such as nodding dogs and furry dice are out, as are strips running cross the top of the windscreen announcing to all that the occupants are an item named Walter and Doris.

What is necessary, however, is a stick-on air freshener on the dashboard (still a word we use, although these days it is more commonly known as the instrument panel - one more backward step under the banner of so-called progress).

Also obligatory is a prominently displayed 'Thank you for not smoking' notice. This will give even more satisfaction if you have recently given up smoking yourself.

To complete the right atmosphere, if a pervading odour of mothballs or menthol can be introduced, you have it.

Now to dress - very important, as always. Remember, you are setting the standard. So with the possible exception of popping down to the corporation tip, always dress the part. Time spent on dressing properly is always worthwhile. Apart from always wanting to look your best, which gives you added respect and authority, any appearance in public should shout out to all observers 'Senior Citizen.'

Dressing for driving is a little bit like getting ready for a formal evening occasion. It is more difficult for the ladies than the men.

For that glitzy night out, the ladies really have to think about their outfit, while the men merely put on their dinner suit.

When travelling by car, the ladies have a similar problem. Smart, functional but never overstated. The men, however, merely don the uniform of the Senior Citizen driver.

This consists of sensible shoes and trousers, shirt, jacket and tie. The jacket ideally should be of a tweed material and to top off the entire ensemble, the obligatory flat cap.

All this is absolutely essential as to anyone driving behind, it immediately indicates that up ahead is a driver of experience, skill, and infinite patience who acts at all times out of the utmost consideration towards other road users. A driver who will never exceed the speed limit and to be absolutely sure will probably drive at a good 10 miles per hour below it. Someone who can also be relied on to show consideration to pedestrians, cyclists and roadside flora and fauna by driving as near to the middle of the road as possible.

But before you can even take to the road, you need to fill up with petrol, and prior to every journey of more than about half a mile, check oil and water.

The trick here is once again to get yourself noticed so that mere mortals can comment on your sense of dress, your bearing, in fact everything you stand for, so they can follow your example.

The best time to call in at a filling station is when it is at its busiest, i.e., early in the morning, or early evening. That is when mums and dads are going to or returning from work, or taking the kids to or from school.

A very good tried and tested way of getting yourself noticed instantly is to approach the petrol pump the wrong way, so that you contrive to be facing in the opposite direction to every other car in the filling station. This will mean that instead of a steady flow of pump users following one behind the other, one lane is blocked until you choose to go, and when you do, you either have to reverse out - which as everyone over 65 knows, is a hazardous, if not impossible manoeuvre at the best of times – or barge your way through at least three other cars, the drivers of which are all behind time to start with.

If additionally you can make one or more of them reverse out, thus causing even more chaos to following motorists, so much the better. You will have achieved your objective. You will have been noticed.

'Look at that well-dressed, well-mannered person in that immaculate car,' they will say.

'He must be a Senior Citizen.'

When you have completed the refuelling part of your visit, move over to the air and water pumps and meticulously inflate each tyre (not forgetting the spare) to the manufacturer's recommended pressures. If this information isn't readily to hand and you have to look it up in the owner's manual, so much the better.

Once again, you should try to pick a time when the filling station is at its busiest with people in a hurry.

Once the tyres have been satisfactorily completed, move on to the water. It shouldn't take too much ingenuity to work out how you can prolong that operation, but if you are struggling, you can use the water supply to wet a cloth and proceed to clean all the windows. or feign not to know where the water filler cap - or even the bonnet release - is located.

For maximum impact, try to select for assistance a youngish man wearing shirt and tie, jacket hanging behind the driver's seat, driving a medium-sized saloon car. Chances are he is a business rep in a hurry.

Now a word about car parking. If you get this right, you can pleasantly pass the best part of half a day.

Where possible, select a car park with a number of vacant spaces. This will give you many options. First, try each one by driving into it forwards, carefully positioning your vehicle exactly between the two white lines. Having achieved this – and with practice, each manoeuvre can take up to ten minutes - try each space again, this time reversing into it.

This will take considerably longer, as you have to use your wing mirrors. This is because by the time you reach Senior Citizen status, lateral movement of the neck is physically impossible. If, before you reverse into the first parking bay, you can arrange to stop your vehicle in order to adjust the wing mirrors, so much the better. This will indicate to any onlookers that even when carrying out the everyday task of parking your car, you tackle the exercise with the same meticulousness, care and attention that the Senior Citizen applies to everything else.

And always remember when you do eventually leave your vehicle, if you are straddling the white line between parking bays, this will ensure that not only will you have plenty of space for easier access into and out of your car, but so too will your neighbours.

If any of you should feel any pang of conscience about taking up more than your allotted space, you can quickly put this out of your mind and salve your conscience by bearing in mind that it is a right that you acquire when you reach Senior Citizen status.

And never forget to have the foresight to arrange your final choice of parking spot so that you have access to the car boot, even though this means that you will have to reverse out into mainstream traffic and the path of pedestrians.

If this manoeuvre is carried out during the rush hour, it can be guaranteed that once again you will have drawn attention to yourself, thus attracting even more favourable comment about the thought, consideration and old-fashioned courtesy shown to others by the Senior Citizen even when performing such an everyday task as parking his car.

Incidentally, the reason for parking to leave easy access to the boot, is that when you return to the car, you will be laden down with goods you have bought today, that you will be taking back for refunds tomorrow. But more about that when we get to shopping.

Two of the greatest dangers on urban roads are the young tearaways who leave traffic lights before they have turned to green at the speed of an Exocet missile, sometimes causing as much devastation; and those drivers who accelerate through the lights just as they are changing to red.

The Senior Citizen, through carefully-controlled driving, can exert a tremendous influence for the good at traffic lights. By waiting until the lights turn fully to green before even thinking of engaging first gear and slowly proceeding across the road junction, you will find that there is probably only time for one car - yours - to get through the lights before they change back to red.

Similarly, if you are approaching traffic lights on green, you will be well aware that they could change to amber without warning at any time, so you will adjust your speed accordingly. This means that as soon as the traffic lights come into view, you will get into second gear as soon as possible and continue at little more than walking pace. This will not only prevent the car behind you shooting the lights as they change to red, it will almost certainly result in you being first in line at every traffic light you pass through, ensuring continued practice of your leisurely getaway.

Fellow road users will lose no time in expressing their true feelings about the consideration of Senior Citizens towards other road users.

One other manoeuvre that is often an indicator of Senior Citizen status is to drive the wrong way down a one-way street. If anyone points out the error of your ways, you point out that you are only going one way, and make a hurried exit at the first opportunity.

Happy motoring – and never forget, this is probably your best opportunity to draw attention to your Senior Citizen status.

EATING OUT

The younger generation may point to the wide selection of restaurants, food and drink from all over the world so freely available today and ask what right have we as Senior Citizens to even offer a comment on the gastronomic revolution that has swept the country over the past decade.

What right have we? And who laid the foundations for this gastronomic revolution?

We did!

Don't you take any of this nouvelle cuisine nonsense from anyone. We invented it.

There were no fancy takeaways when we were young – fish, chips and mushy peas and that was it. It was even considered revolutionary in some quarters for the chip shop to sell pies and puddings, let alone curry sauce and giant sausages.

When you went into a pub, there was no way you would be handed a menu thicker than a telephone directory. Pie or pickled egg, that was the choice.

But once free of the shackles of post war austerity, we certainly pushed back the barriers of good living.

Nobody had ever heard of wine until we took that first tentative sip of sauternes as we savoured the delights of a prawn cocktail.

And whose generation was it that gave the world chicken in a basket? Schooners of sherry? Tea bags?

There would be no such thing as Asian, Bengalese, Chinese, Greek, Indian, Italian, Thai, Turkish, Tibetan or any other type of restaurant if we had not fashioned such a firm foundation on which to build this world-wide cross section of culinary creativity.

So it is important whenever you are out dining to let everyone else know that they are in the presence of a Senior Citizen, without whose endorsement they would not have been enjoying their palate-teasing experience.

As with any other aspect of Senior Citizenship, there are certain giveaway signs that such a person of high esteem and gastronomic experience is around. Senior Citizens always wipe the chairs before they sit down, and the tables as soon as they are seated. This is because these days, many members of the younger generation, with their tattoos, body piercing and lack of suitable clothing, may have just come back from foreign parts where they could have picked up anything.

They will also move tables at least twice before finally settling on one they consider to be satisfactory.

And the Senior Citizen has helped to keep prices down to a reasonable level by always displaying a   high degree of thrift when dining out. There is no way we are going to throw money away on overpriced meals and drinks. After the hardships we had to endure during our formative years, there is no way we are going to throw money away on anything. This thrift is not to be confused, incidentally, with tightfistedness, which applies to many people, but never the Senior Citizen.

So a lifetime of experience has left its mark. When it comes to saving money, there are no equals. And to help you maintain this time-honoured tradition, here are a few quick tips on how to eat and drink out cheaply.

If you wish to have a pot of tea for two, order a pot for one, ask for extra hot water and help yourself to an extra cup and saucer.

If one of you wants tea and the other coffee, order the coffee, extra hot water and use your own teabag. If you can remember to carry round with you a small leak-proof plastic bag, you will be able to keep the teabag and use it several more times before it has outlived its usefulness.

If your budget stretches to a cake as well, test the freshness by sticking your finger firmly into it, explaining that they don't use the same ingredients today as they did in your day, and nothing is ever as fresh as it was. (Note: Having established that the cake is fresh, don't take the one you have just fingered).

Senior Citizens often eat out (lunchtime is cheaper than evening) because they may as well use someone else's heat, light and cooking facilities, thus saving on their own bills.

The obvious way of saving money is to go for the two for one offers available at many pubs.

You could save more by asking for children's portions, explaining that your appetite isn't what it was.

You can also save money by asking for just one meal and an extra plate, and dividing the food between the two of you when it arrives; or go for the cheapest option of all – a children's portion between the two of you. Never pay more than you need to.

If you are on your own, you will probably find that pro rata, the two for one offer is cheaper than buying one dish individually. Order the two for one offer, and get them to plate up the other meal so you can take it home to either have later or freeze for another day. (Don' forget to return the plate when you go back for your next helping, as failing to do so may get Senior Citizens everywhere a bad name).

And finally, one golden rule for Senior Citizens everywhere. Never order anything from a menu if you can't pronounce it.

EDUCATION

Although you may never have passed an examination in your life, let alone been within spitting distance of a University or College of Further Education, you are more than qualified to educate those younger than yourself because you have gained your knowledge in that highest of academic institutions, the University of Life.

You will know, of course, that since you were at school, standards have fallen considerably.

It may be argued that this is not so, and many statistics will be trotted out to prove it. But don't you believe any of it. Disputing facts and statistics is not only a prerogative of the Senior Citizen, but a duty.

Each year, more and more young people are leaving schools and colleges with more and more O levels, A levels, GCSEs, HNDs and NVQs. Don't be fooled into believing that it as a result of improved educational standards, a greater willingness on the part of the young to take advantage of the opportunities offered, or that they are just plain brighter than previous generations.

The truth is that the exams are easier than they were in our day. Far easier. This is obvious because as everyone knows, no one is as widely educated or better qualified to give advice on any subject under the sun than the Senior Citizen.

Another point to bear in mind when confronted by anyone under 30 with a fistful of paper qualifications, is just how useful they are in practice.

Information Technology, Media Studies, Human Resources - we never had such things in our day, because we never needed them. We had a fair grounding in the three Rs and that was good enough to carry us through life.

What good is a degree in Information Technology to anyone, if they're not capable of stripping down and rebuilding a motor bike in the hall?

How far will your Media Studies degree get you in life if you are incapable of mending your own shoes?

As for Human Resources - a lot of use that is if you're totally incapable of giving your drains a good rodding when the need arises.

If it wasn't for the constant diligence of our generation, a lot of the traditional skills essential to the smooth running of life would have already disappeared.

Black-leading the grate, dyeing old clothes to give them a few more years useful life, hand-weaving a peg rug.

You have a tremendous responsibility in keeping these traditions alive for future generations. Showing the youngsters of today how much more satisfying it can be to spend months making your own fireside rug out of torn up strips of old clothing woven into a piece of sacking instead of just wandering into a shop and buying one; how much more satisfying it can be to get up on a cold winter's morning and start the day by raking out your fire grate instead of having instant heat at the touch of a button.

Think University of Life whenever you are faced with anything that smacks remotely of modern living, and help create a better future for mankind.

ENTERTAINMENT

Now here is a subject we really do know something about.

Music hall, repertory theatre, ballroom dancing, the big band sound – we had it all. What have they got today? Mindless noise.

Soul music, rap, heavy metal, garage music – what's all that about? It's either music or it isn't, and we all know the answer to that one.

Was Ivor Novello into heavy metal? Was Noel Coward a rap artiste? No way.

There was nothing finer than to hear a true artiste whistling In a Monastery Garden or playing Any Old Iron on the spoons.

We would sit riveted in the music hall as a budgie pulled a little cart along a table top, or a scantily-clad young lady stood on one hand on an inflated ball, whirling hoops round her ankles. That was the true meaning of artistry.

But perhaps where we excelled most was in entertaining ourselves at home.

Every time there was a family get-together, we'd be round the piano singing all the old tunes. We'd be playing all the party games that broke the ice, got people to relax, enjoy themselves.

So next time you find yourself at a young person's party, where the majority of the guests are jigging about meaninglessly to some unidentifiable, deafening dirge, while a disc jockey goes berserk spinning his records and yelling into a microphone, you take charge of proceedings. Get your old records out, announce that the next dance will be a Veleta and after supper, you can all play pinning the tail on the donkey, spinning the bottle, or truth or consequence.

I can guarantee the party guests will gaze at you in shocked admiration, as they unanimously agree that it has taken a Senior Citizen to show them what entertainment is really all about.

FAIRMINDEDNESS

For Senior Citizen, read Elder Statesman. Camp Elder, Head of the Tribe. However you describe it, it all adds up to the same. You are the one who is looked up to, has the wisdom and experience to make unbiased judgement, to lead by example.

Fairmindedness is a bye word of the Senior Citizen. Show people that you are capable of seeing everyone's point of view, that your life is ruled by courtesy and understanding, that your sole aim in life is to be unscrupulously fair at all times in your judgement of others – providing they agree with your point of view.

The rest are not worth bothering with. There is no way you are going to break down the prejudices of someone who is stubborn, arrogant and holds a different opinion to yourself.

FAMILY

This is where Senior Citizens really come into their own.

They created their family. It all started with their union. They are the ones on whom their dynasty has been founded and on whose values it will continue to thrive.

Anyone wondering where the boundary line falls between helpful and constructive advice and interfering - or sticking one's beak in, as it is often referred to by those who know no better - shouldn't dwell on the subject for too long.

The short answer is that there isn't one, certainly as far as you are concerned. Every word you utter falls into the helpful and constructive advice category.

The giving of advice and assistance so selflessly and freely is borne out of the adage mother (or grandmother) knows best. This isn't an issue for debate, it is a fact. Nor is it sexist not to mention father or grandfather. They usually try to keep as low a profile as possible.

Every Senior Citizen knows that their children are completely incapable of bringing up children of their own.

If you have grandchildren, you have special responsibilities to ensure that these innocent mites are not influenced by that lost generation to which their parents belong. In other words, if your children took not a jot of notice of your well-intentioned advice, which is more than likely, you must make doubly sure that your grandchildren do.

Dietary requirements are an alien culture to young people today, and the need to educate themselves and their families to spend wisely, save wisely, and live a life of prudence seems to have passed them by completely.

Any thoughts that children and family come first are greeted with disbelief.

They have no time for them; they spoil them because it is easier to buy them off than to spend quality time with them; they feed them all the wrong things.

They will argue, of course, that in spite of this, the children of today are in the main leaner, fitter, more intelligent than their parents were at that age and dramatically more so than their grandparents were. But that shouldn't stop you from insisting that you know best. You do. No doubt about it.

For you to be able to exert most influence, it is useful to live fairly close to the target of your goodwill, so that contact can be made at least twice a week. This way, more opportunities for giving advice will present themselves. If you don't live close enough to do this, the answer is simple. Move.

'You're not sending him to school in that. He'll freeze to death.'

'They'll never know what their legs are for if you run them everywhere in the car.'

'She shouldn't be having that until she's eaten her dinner'.

'Those children watch too much television.'

'Computer games didn't exist in my day. You had to make your own amusement.'

These are just a few of the gems of advice that every self-respecting Senior Citizen will be familiar with, even though for the most part they fall on deaf ears. And don't be put off by pleas of having to make the tea, do the washing, do the ironing, clean the house. We managed to get it all done and we didn't have any help. And don't even think of entertaining the 'have to work' argument.

They don't have to take a paid job. They don't need the money. Their place is at home with the children.

And definitely don't entertain ' I'm entitled to a life as well, you know'. Any claim they had to a life of their own flew out of the window when the first born arrived.

Your children make totally unsuitable parents, and you have a moral duty to make sure that your grandchildren are brought up to appreciate the finer things of life - namely all the values held in such esteem by yourself and held in such contempt by their parents.

FINANCES

'Hire purchase! Hire <u>purchase</u>! There was no such thing in our day. If you couldn't pay for it, you couldn't have it. You did without.'

How many times have you had cause to come out with these immortal words when talking to your offspring? And do they listen? No way.

Because they are subject to forces beyond their control. Forces that bombard them daily with promises of untold riches, wealth beyond their wildest dreams, material fulfilment that was unimaginable at the same stage in our lives.

And it is all down to a small rectangle of plastic. It's all so easy. When you have reached your limit on one, there is always another.

But the reason we can say without any fear of contradiction that all this was unimaginable at the same stage in our lives is because it wasn't available. Because the powers that be in banking circles knew it would have been a total waste of time trying to tempt us. We were nowhere near as gullible as today's young folk.

We knew there was no such thing as a free lunch. If there was a land of milk and honey, it was a long, painful journey to reach it. So we didn't even take the first faltering steps down that route, thank you very much.

It is your duty, fellow missionaries, to preach to the young the error of their ways.

If you wanted a car, you waited until you could afford it. It may have taken you years. So long, in fact, that when you were able to afford it, you could no longer enjoy it. But what you did enjoy was the deep feeling of satisfaction of knowing that it was paid for. Every penny.

Look at the young today. As soon as they learn to drive, they are flashing round the roads in the latest sports car, with ear-splitting sound system, in their designer clothes, expensive haircuts, sunglasses welded to the tops of their heads. They probably paid more for their shades than we did for our first car!

On the surface, they seem to have everything. But don't be fooled. They get their unbelievable aura of self confidence from their material possessions.

What kind of life is that? They can't possibly be happy with their lot. Not deep down.

So don't miss an opportunity to point out how things were when you were younger – and how much more happiness you got out of life.

When your offspring announces they are moving into a penthouse flat you tell them that when you were their age you had a two up and two down with an outside loo. Paper was a luxury and you had to be a good singer, as there was no lock on the door.

But you were happy.

When you visit them and they're watching their 50 inch plasma TV screen which occupies best part of one wall, with its surround sound, point out that when you were their age television was an alien word to you. You reckoned you were lucky to own a wireless the size of a fridge that got two programmes.

But you were happy.

And when they come back from Mauritius, where they've spent most of the winter, you tell them when you were their age, you were lucky to get a week in a Cleethorpes boarding house sharing a bathroom with three other families.

But you were happy.

It is your bounden duty to get them to realise what we have known all our lives. Money is the root of all evil.

Especially when other people have it, and you don't.

GARDEN CENTRES

Garden centres, practically unrecognisable to what they were a generation ago when most of them went under the names of market gardens, are playing an increasingly important role in the life of the Senior Citizen.

They are so comprehensive these days with their wide range of indoor and outdoor displays, they can provide a colourful day out for the Senior Citizen – and most important, entrance is free and so, too, is the parking.

Couple that with the added advantage that most garden centres usually boast a very presentable coffee shop, with a wide variety of dishes available all day at competitive prices, and the Senior Citizen is practically on his holidays.

Garden centres are light, airy and colourful. While the younger generation are recounting their holiday in some exotic location with all the colour of the native flora, you can find it all in the local garden centre. There is no long wait at an airport to get there, no passport required and no currency problems. You don't need any special vaccinations or insurance.

If you're looking for temperatures in the 80s – no problem. Just move into the heated greenhouse.

If full board is your style, you can chomp your way through full English or continental breakfast on arrival, crumpets and coffee mid-morning, an appetising savoury snack at lunchtime and afternoon tea. True, the majority don't do evening meals, but who needs an evening meal after that lot?

Of course, some Senior Citizens do actually enjoy gardening, and they can buy all manner of equipment to make this task more pleasurable, together with an array of plants that will add colour to the drabbest plot.

But for those of you who are not so keen, but who wish to give the impression that not only are you as physically active as ever, but are an expert in all things horticultural, it is important that you make your presence felt every time you visit your local garden centre without actually spending any money.

To do this you pick the largest trolley available and proceed to load it with fertiliser for the lawn, shrubs, trees, bushes, sprays for discouraging every animal and insect known to man and enough boxes of plants to restock the best part of Kew Gardens.

Try to pick a really busy day, so you can be seen by the most people. You may be able to go on any day of the week, but Sunday is usually best.

And don't fall for any days where there is a discount for pensioners. This may save money but it is hardly likely to brand you as an affluent person who puts more value on the appearance of your garden than anything as mundane as cash.

Having filled your trolley to the admiration of everyone who is around to see you, you find a quiet spot to park it and make a hurried exit.

You will also get a lot of satisfaction from the knowledge that you have more than likely created a job for a hitherto unemployed youngster, who will have been taken on solely to replace all the products that Senior Citizens leave around.

You will have struck a telling blow with a double-sided blade. You will have once again made the influence of the Senior Citizen well and truly felt, while saving at least one young person from a life of crawling out of bed at mid-day, living off state benefits and ruining their eyesight by playing computer games every waking hour.

If you should be eventually rumbled by a vigilant member of staff, you can always fall back on the age old get-out for Senior Citizens everywhere.

When challenged, you look your adversary squarely in the eye and say ' Who are you? Who am I? How did I get here? Nurse. <u>Nurse!</u>

HEALTH CLUBS

A healthy body and a healthy mind are the keys to a long and active life. You know this, of course. You have only managed to survive this long by keeping your body and brain in prime condition.

So here, your responsibilities are two-fold – to continue to maintain your own body and mind in peak condition; and to mount a crusade to promote the healthy body/healthy mind philosophy to those unfortunate enough not to have hitherto received the message.

This basically means the majority of under 60s, and in particular those under 25, the majority of whom have sadly been led astray by having their lives controlled by drugs and alcohol, as any Senior Citizen will tell you.

An effective way of spreading the word on fitness is to join a health club.

And don't be deviated from your purpose by the sight of lithe, fit young bodies working out at your fitness centre. These people are in the minority and have no doubt been planted there in a desperate attempt to undermine the Senior Citizen's campaign to spread the word that your way of life is the only way forward if civilisation is to stand even an outside chance of surviving the next Century, never mind the next Millenium.

It is a fact that everyone – except Senior Citizens - who use a health club are either recovering from something, or about to get something.

They are doing workouts to strengthen weakened muscles, recover from an operation or train so vigorously that within days of joining they are heading for A & E at the local hospital.

You must set an example. Health clubs are places to be enjoyed, to meet your friends and generally relax. So the first thing to do is avoid any piece of equipment that even hints at physical exertion.

Once you have changed into all the right gear for the gym – this is essential if you wish to be taken seriously – make your way to the track, where you have arranged to meet any friends and acquaintances - preferably at least three others. Don't go anywhere. Just chat, exchange pleasantries and generally relax for about 10 minutes. This will effectively interrupt any serious training by anyone who is trying to power walk, jog or run, thus minimising their risk of pulling any muscles.

You then move on to four of the more vigorous exercise machines. Cross trainers are a good area. You each mount a machine, then just stand their chatting for another 20 minutes

When you have completed your stint on the cross trainers, move on to the rowing machines, and do exactly the same. It not only ensures that you don't do yourself any physical injury, but as no one else can use those particular machines for the duration of your occupancy, you are saving at least four other folk from the dire consequences of over-exercise.

Finally the warm down. You all make your way back to the track where you set off at a gentle stroll with your friends, strung out across the four lanes. If your earlier tactic stopped a number of people from over-exerting themselves on the track, this one is guaranteed to bring all activity to a complete stop.

If you feel particularly energetic, you can finish your session by lying in the hydro pool close enough to the steps to stop anyone else getting in. Then you go home, totally satisfied that you have done your bit helping prevent those younger and more foolish than you doing irreparable damage to their bodies by over-exercising.

IMAGE

This is a very important part of the Senior Citizen's make-up. There is absolutely no chance of being taken seriously unless you project the correct image.

Bearing in mind the importance of the first impression, aim to create at first glance an image of someone who is to be trusted, confided in, admired and looked up to.

Adopt an air of authority and self-confidence. Be self-assured but not overbearing.

How you should dress is dealt with under the DRESS section of this guide.

And don't forget to wear that most important accessory, particularly when meeting and greeting strangers – a smile.

As you pass complete strangers in the street, walking perfectly erect, dressed as if you were going to a Royal garden party, look them straight in the eye and sport a grin on your face as wide as the M6. I can guarantee that you will not go unnoticed.

JUGGLING AGES

Age is a funny thing. When you are 10, you want everyone to think you are a teenager. When you are 15, you want everyone to think you are 18. When you are 65, you don't mind anyone knowing it. It is a milestone – and a birthday it is difficult to keep to yourself anyway.

But there are some circumstances under which your memory can play strange tricks when it comes to age.

Sixty-five in the right company can become late fifties – or if the young man or young lady is sufficiently interested, early fifties.

Similarly, 70 becomes early sixties, 75 late 60s – but it is after this that things become more difficult, because one of the essentials of being a good liar about anything, never mind age, is that you need a good memory. And as we all know three things happen as we get older – firstly, your memory starts to go and I can' remember the other two.

So once we get beyond a certain age – and this varies with the individual – there is more kudos in making out that you are older than you are.

Get past 70, and the muscles in your face sag to the point of giving you a vacant expression, and you may well admit to being nearly eighty. Make 80, and you will tell folk that you are nearly 90, always in the expectation that they will say 'You never are'.

Once they stop saying that, give up. You're on a loser anyway.

JUSTIFYING ACTIONS/WORDS

This is something that the non-Senior Citizen has to do – never you.

Whatever you say or do, no matter how bizarre it may seem to others, it is built on a lifetime of experience and achievement, and is therefore perfectly acceptable behaviour.

Any tendency towards eccentricity has absolutely nothing to do with the fact that you are getting on a bit and your mind isn't what it used to be.

Unless, of course, you are caught leaving Tesco with a frozen chicken stuffed down your drawers.

KEEPSAKES

Perhaps no subject evokes more feeling than the differing attitudes of the Senior Citizen and their young offspring towards keepsakes, or heirlooms as we prefer to call them.

We are of a generation that knew that practically everything we possessed would be worth a small fortune one day.

That is why we threw nothing away – unlike the throwaway society of today.

But what can you expect? Everything they buy is in a throwaway container.

They never had to wash a milk bottle and return it so it could be re-used.

They never had to make a walkie-talkie for the kids out of two tin lids and a piece of string. They have mobile phones today, don't they? Which many of them change more often than their socks.

How many times have you taken your offspring up into the loft and told them 'One day, all this will be yours?'

And how many of them, as they surveyed the broken kettle without a plug, the pot dog with a leg missing that you won at the fairground at Blackpool, or the one-bar electric fire uttered so much as a 'Thank you.'

But one day they will thank you for collecting all these heirlooms. Thank you for passing them on to them. Not for the value – when it comes to that aspect of it, they are probably right. The lot is worthless.

But they will have a loft of their own. And in today's throwaway society, what will they have to put in it, unless you leave them enough stuff to give them a head start?

So carry on collecting – one man's rubbish is another man's heirloom – or, in the case of your own family, vice versa.

LEISURE TIME

When it comes to leisure time, the most important thing to impress on folk is that it is something other people have – never yourself.

When you have worked all your life, brought up a family, cared for a partner, taken a responsible, caring role in society towards others, you've never had a minute to yourself.

If you are caught sneaking off to the cinema or a theatre, it is so you can tell your friends what the film is about so they won't waste their money going if they don't fancy it.

If you go to a concert, it is only to get a copy of the programme for old Mrs Smithers who likes to read about these things.

Going on holiday is something you do for the benefit of your partner or family – 'couldn't be bothered, myself. No time. But he/she/they needed a break so I had to go with them.'

LOVE

This is an old fashioned word and one of the only two four-letter words that were part of our vocabulary in our younger days, the other one being work.

The young generation today don't know the meaning of love – lust is the nearest they get to it.

Love means affection, caring, sharing, taking a delight in being part of each other's lives. It may be becoming rapidly outmoded amongst today's youngsters, but it carried us through some hard times. When we fell in love, it was for ever. Not for five minutes, as seems to be the norm these days. We stuck by our families in thick and thin. We sweated to bring them up, give them a decent standard of living and a good start in life.

More often than not, it was a sacrifice. We had to tighten our belts, go without ourselves. But we never complained. We did it out of love. L-o-v-e. It was the word on which our generation was built. We survived wars, unemployment, shortages because we were solidly welded together by love. Love for our families, love for our friends and love for our fellow beings.

Without a rekindling of this basic of feelings among today's youth, there is no hope for the future. Mankind will transgress into a snarling, aggressive, arrogant offshoot of the animal kingdom.

If you can make one young person a day aware of the infinite advantages of true love, you will be doing your bit to help make the world a better place for everyone.

So, dear Senior Citizen, at every opportunity it is up to you to put across the message that love triumphs over all adversity, and the way to demonstrate this is to walk hand in hand with your loved one whenever you are out together.

This public display of your eternal affection for and trust in each other will send a strong, clear message to passing teenagers that love is not a word to be ashamed of.

Some may even be so moved by your public demonstration of togetherness that they will break off sending text messages on their mobile phones long enough to observe to their friends 'Look at that wonderful display of trust and affection. I certainly think we can learn from the example of those Senior Citizens who are so obviously in love.'

MANNERS

Again, something that you were born with, but others seem to have totally missed out on.

As the woman in the queue for the till at the supermarket elbows her way in front of you – it will be a young woman, in all probability, as our generation wouldn't do any such thing – point out to her that good manners cost nothing and attract far more admiration than bad manners.

You will probably find, as she whistles through the hole in her nose where the safety pin usually goes when she is dressed formally, that she will be deeply grateful to you for pointing this out, apologise for her temporary lapse and allow you to take your rightful place at the head of the queue.

No matter what form any display of bad manners takes, firmly but gently point out the error of the culprit's ways. Because these days it is so easy to take the easy way out and put it down to the fact that they know no better and are beyond redemption – particularly if the offending person happens to be six feet six inches tall and built like a piece of earth-moving equipment.

You will find more often than not that any display of bad manners – again by someone younger than yourself - is a temporary lapse and one that the offender is happy for you to point out.

Before doing so, however, a word of warning. You will find, as many of us do once we reach Senior Citizen status, that the young people of today have adopted a language all their own that bears little resemblance to the Queen's English we were taught.

So before challenging anyone who transgresses that thin line between acceptable and unacceptable behaviour, it may well be worth your while to increase you vocabulary by learning as many two word retorts as you can, the second word being 'off'.

Your actions may not get you added to their Christmas card list, but you can be certain that they will definitely not go unnoticed.

MORAL JUDGEMENT

You haven't got where you are today without the strongest sense of what is right and what is wrong. Much of the trouble in the world is rooted in the fact that the majority of people – particularly the young – do not know right from wrong, have no sense of justice, virtue or compassion and when it comes to judging the morals of others, are definitely non-starters.

Our generation is at a definite advantage, here. We were born knowing the difference between right and wrong.

Granted, we didn't always abide by the rules. Occasionally we may have strayed far enough from the moral path into the fringes of lawlessness. But we always knew where the line was drawn, and if we ever did cross it, you can be sure it was merely an act of high spirits that had temporarily clouded our judgment. Unlike the youngsters of today who spend most of their miserable lives outside the law because they know no better.

So whenever you get the chance to point out the rights and wrongs of a situation, seize it eagerly with both hands. Whenever you come across someone younger than yourself on the verge of giving in to temptation – particularly where the sins of the flesh are concerned, as this seems to be the area that is at the centre of today's moral decline – explain to them that this is not the stuff of true character and upright citizenship.

It will make them stop and think. 'This is the advice of a Senior Citizen. A fine, upstanding person who has led a blameless life because they have moral fibre, know right from wrong and have laid down the pattern for a better way of life for generations to come.'

It will take courage, dear friend, particularly if the subject of your attention is one of a group, it is late at night and alcohol has been taken in abundant quantities.

But remember, your actions could have a tremendous impact on the lives of two young people who may otherwise have plunged headlong into the abyss of degradation by one single abandoned act which they will regret for the rest of their lives.

Your actions could also have a tremendous impact on your own life, possibly shortening it considerably if you choose the wrong time, place and subject for your lecture on moral standards.

NATIONAL TRUST

The advantages to a Senior Citizen of being a member of the National Trust, once you have paid your subscription, are very similar to those to be found in a garden centre.

You enjoy free parking, all-day catering, a wide variety of well-kept homes and grounds – and, most important to the Senior Citizen, somewhere to go when it's raining.

And just as you can impress onlookers in the garden centre with your vast knowledge of your subject by what you buy; as a member of the National Trust you can command equal respect by your knowledge of the properties, all of which you glean from the room stewards and guides.

You take a tour of the house/hall/mansion, and in every room you have a quiet chat with the room steward to find out as much as you can about that area.

When you have completed your tour, you go back into the house and start again, stopping before you enter each room, waiting for a reasonable group of people then discussing with your companion the room you are about to enter in the greatest detail. This never fails to impress.

If you can time your discussion to coincide with the arrival of a guided tour, and spike the guns of the guide before they go into their piece, so much the better.

If, in spite of your efforts, you still fail to get yourself noticed, get yourself on a guided tour and resort to Plan B – at frequent intervals during the commentary, in a loud, clear voice, utter the battle cry of the Senior Citizen – 'What did he say, dear?'

NEW IDEAS

There are none. It's all been done before by our generation.

Never a day goes by without some claim or other for a breakthrough in one thing or another, some technological development or a revolutionary way of doing something.

Forget it. They only <u>think</u> they've found a new way of doing things and it's only a matter of time before they realise it.

It is a great temptation to smile smugly and say 'I told you so.' But this isn't the way of the Senior Citizen. Never mock those without your wisdom and foresight. Take the benevolent view. Not everyone is as worldly wise or as far-sighted as the Senior Citizen.

There are times when the cause can best be served by maintaining a dignified silence.

This is one of those times.

NUTRITION

You can't beat good, wholesome food. You can't argue with that.

What you can argue with is what constitutes good wholesome food. And on this subject, there is no contest. The Senior Citizen is definitely always right. You only have to look at us – lean, fit, virile and mentally sharp as a tack.

Good basic produce. Meat and two veg. None of your fancy stuff. Plain and simple, that was our philosophy. We didn't need an army of TV chefs to tell us how to make a meal appetising. And we didn't need any of these fancy fruits and vegetables from all over the world. If it couldn't be grown on the allotment, it had no place in our diet.

There were no such people as nutritionists in our day. We knew instinctively what was good for us and what wasn't.

And we knew how to cook it. None of your microwaves for us. If you couldn't boil it, fry it or roast it there was no way it would find its way into our digestive system.

And there was no waste. Collect the fat, use it again. Serve the left- overs up cold the next day, or chuck them in the soup.

There was none of this nonsense talk about salt and sugar and fat being bad for you in our day. My granddad liked nothing better than a plate of chips fried in beef dripping smothered in salt and vinegar, and a big fat chocolate éclair all washed down with a mug of tea with four sugars, and it didn't do him any harm.

He lived to be nearly thirty-five!

So when the younger generation go droning on about healthy eating and healthy lifestyles, you point out the downside.

It's only since all these modern fads about healthy eating and healthy lifestyles came in that so many folk need new teeth and hip replacements.

Nutrition? They know nothing.

OLD AGE

Something that applies to other people – never yourself.

OLD DAYS

This is a period in history, like the stone age, that is part of mankind's heritage and it is your duty to ensure that it is a period that is never forgotten.

If you feel it may be a tall order to try to recall the old days at every conceivable opportunity in just about every conversation, just bear one fact in mind and the rest will come naturally.

In the old days, everything was better than it is today.

Money went further, relationships were stronger, quality of life was infinitely better.

So when you are taken out in your son's new car, with eight speaker stereo system, satellite navigation and air conditioning, never miss a chance to remind him that it was never like that in the old days.

Cars today may be stacked with gimmicks - a thousand and one things you never knew you needed. The result? A thousand and one more reasons for something to go wrong.

We may have shivered in our old boneshaker with no heater. We may have been off work for a week with back trouble after wielding the starting handle on a cold morning. But we were better off than they are today – far better off. Because in those days they knew how to build a car. In the old days, you didn't have to change it every two years. It was good for 20 at least.

When you visit your offspring's new house, just look at the quality of the workmanship, the finish. Can't hold a candle to the standards we were used to.

They may boast master bedrooms with fitted wardrobes, en suite bathrooms and whirlpool baths. But it's all top show. What matters is the substance of the building. And in the old days, did they know how to build a house.

They don't make wood today like they used to. You tell them.

Practically every aspect of life provides an opportunity for you to regale anyone who will listen with tales of how things were better in the old days – particularly if you have a family with young children.

In the old days, children were better behaved because they knew their place. Clothes would last for generations. Schools were better. That's obvious when you bear in mind that most of us left at 15 or 16. We obviously knew all we needed to know by then. We didn't have to spend another five years at some sixth form college or university before we were ready to face the outside world.

In the old days, life was a dream. There was no crime and the sun shone every day of the week from the end of March to the end of October.

British summertime really meant summertime.

So spare a thought for the youngsters of today, who will never be able to look back on the good old days, because to be able to look back on the good old days, you have to create some good old days to look back on.

And there is no chance of that with the youngsters of today.

They're far too busy enjoying themselves.

PATIENCE AND UNDERSTANDING

Patience is one of the Senior Citizen's greatest virtues.

It is expected that with your long and full experience of life, you will take your time. You will look at life's little challenges from every aspect so that when you do reach a decision, it is one based on all known facts.

Inevitably this will mean that people younger and less experienced of life than yourself may construe any lack of haste to respond on your part as vagueness, even the onset of senility. This is only to be expected of a generation with so little time to appreciate the finer things in life. So little time to even notice the flowers, let alone smell them.

It is up to you to show them the error of their ways. That the only way to cope effectively with the speed of life today is to put the brake on, slow down and proceed at a pace that is comfortable to you.

Don't rush, don't make any snap decisions, proceed through life with a serenity that truly reflects the infinite patience of the Senior Citizen.

One of the best opportunities to put this into practice presents itself every time you find yourself at the head of a very long queue at the supermarket check- out.

Politely refuse the offer of help with the packing, telling the check-out assistant that you are more than capable of doing it yourself. Don't rush. It's bad for your blood pressure. The fact that your leisurely approach to the task in hand won't do anything for the blood pressure of the other people in the queue is not your problem.

You will not fail to notice the people in the queue behind you smiling in admiration, which, to the casual observer, could be erroneously construed at first glance as muttering through clenched teeth.

As you walk away from the check out, watching the cashier putting up the 'Cash Point Closed' notice as she goes off for a quick nervous breakdown, you can go on your way happy in the knowledge that you have enriched so many lives by your fine example of living life at the pace it is supposed to be lived.

The pace of the Senior Citizen.

PROPERTY

Senior Citizens don't have homes. They don't live in flats, apartments, semis, detached houses or country mansions.

They have property.

Property can be any or all of the above. You may have a modest one - bedroom flat in the most unfashionable area of town, but the very word property evokes visions of a stately pile to rival Chatsworth.

So whenever the subject of where you live arises, always use the words 'I have a property in…'

Unless, that is, you do happen to own a stately pile to rival Chatsworth – in which case, for Heaven's sake, say so.

QUALIFICATIONS

Always a useful tool when asserting your authority as a Senior Citizen.

Professional qualifications, technical qualifications – anything you can think of. And if you have to invent the odd qualification or letters after your name, go ahead - the more bizarre the better. This way, you are never likely to be drawn into conversation by someone who is likely to have the same qualification – but genuine, in their case.

As you know, when it comes to further education there is no substitute for the University of Life, and you should point this out whenever appropriate. But there will be occasions when you are in the company of genuine scholars, and if you are to maintain credibility, you may have to match degree for degree.

If the talk is of O levels, don't plump for 12. Six is an ideal number. It reduces the chances of being caught out in a subject you haven't the vaguest idea about by 50 per cent. (If you worked that one out for yourself, claiming a mathematics O level could be a safe bet).

And remember, it is not always quantity but frequently quality that counts.

Four As and two Bs should establish your credentials nicely. Similarly, when it comes to A levels., three or four are more than adequate. Again, grades are important and three A's and a B should be suitably impressive.

You can of course say anything you like. No one is going to ask you for proof and no one is going to check up on you. The only person who can pull the rug from under your feet is yourself – by professing to know everything about a subject that you even have difficulty spelling.

So before mentioning your specialised subjects, try to find out something about whoever you happen to be discussing the subject with. This way, you will hopefully be able to avoid any subject that they are expert in.

If you are unsure, always stick to subjects that are fairly general, such as English, Maths, Geography and History. If you try to be clever and throw in an A grade in the economic history of Poland, you can guarantee that you will one day bump into a former Polish Chancellor who will quickly blow your cover.

Of course, all this guidance is only for use in exceedingly desperate circumstances, as one thing the Senior Citizen absolutely abhors is telling lies.

Bending the truth, however, isn't quite the same thing.

A first at Oxford could be anything from a first class return ticket to a first class stamp. But it is a great conversation stopper when you come to be talking education.

RECREATION

To the uninitiated, recreation could be confused with leisure time.

What nonsense, as any Senior Citizen will tell you.

Leisure is a time for taking things easy when you are not otherwise occupied, for relaxing when you find yourself with time on your hands.

Senior Citizens never have time on their hands. They work relentlessly to ensure that the world never falls prey to the follies of the suicide squad – the young. There is most definitely no such thing as leisure time in the Senior Citizen's lifestyle.

Recreation, on the other hand, is totally different. It is absolutely essential in promoting a healthy mind and body through the pursuit of an enjoyable activity or two. An essential tool in the honing of that fine art of Senior Citizenship.

And there are numerous activities to choose from - some more active than others.

Some require no more physical exertion than pressing a button or two on the TV remote control, or holding a newspaper - activities that are an essential part of the Senior Citizen's lifestyle in the constant quest to keep up with current trends, thus adding credence to any discussion in which they may find themselves involved.

Picture an evening at the Ferret and Firkin, where conversation turns to the match on TV last night. The seasoned Senior Citizen will, at the first opportunity, not only voice his opinion on the match, but offer a wide range of comments on every aspect of the game, from the dubious parentage of the referee to the eyesight problems of the linesman. Anyone in earshot will look on in admiration.

'This Senior Citizen certainly knows what he is talking about when it comes to sport,' they will tell each other.

'He must be equally well versed in just about everything.'

For those who prefer a more active take on recreation, there is the card table, the bowling green or the bingo hall.

Playing bridge or whist is popular. These are supposedly friendly games where you arrive with a close friend, face each other all afternoon or evening in tight-lipped silence, and leave not speaking to each other only to say as you go your separate ways how much you enjoyed yourselves and 'See you at the same time next week'.

The bowling green can be a pleasant outdoor venue where you can enjoy the company of like-minded people, but bear in mind the amount of bending involved. It is definitely not a pursuit for anyone who once down there needs the services of an osteopath or a block and tackle to get upright again.

While for those with a leaning towards advanced mathematics, there is the weekly visit to the local bingo hall.

All these activities provide excellent opportunities for recharging your batteries and spreading the word at the same time. But they provide little scope for reaching your target audience – the young and foolish, because the aforementioned activities tend to be supported in the main by Senior Citizens anyway, so you are preaching to what should be the converted.

So to achieve maximum impact with your teachings, you need to concentrate more on activities where the participation of younger people is encouraged, but which will not put too much physical strain on you. And to this end, cricket and golf fill the bill perfectly – cricket as a spectator and golf as a participant.

The county cricket ground on the occasion of a one day match is an ideal venue. It is this format that attracts the younger spectator in large numbers, thus providing a wider audience for your views about everything.

But first of all, you have to establish your credentials. Make it crystal clear to everyone around that here is a Senior Citizen. There are a number of ways you can do this, but the one favoured by the majority seems to be to arrive in good time, pick a row with only one person on it, preferably with a bag or briefcase that he has placed on the seat next to him. This is the seat that you make for.

You ask the spectator to remove his bag so you can sit down. He will probably point out that every other seat in the row is free. Which is exactly what you want. Because this gives you the opportunity to forcibly tell him and anyone else within earshot that this is your regular seat and even if the ground was empty, you would still expect to sit there.

This will impress the other spectator no end. In one simple sentence you will have established that you are a regular, so you know everything there is to know about cricket; that you command enough respect to have the same seat every time you turn up for a match; and you will have exerted your authority as a Senior Citizen – an excellent base from which to regale him on any subject under the sun in the certain knowledge not only that he will hang on every word, but feel honoured that you have chosen to sit next to him.

He will move to another seat after a while, where you will probably see him chatting to his new neighbours and pointing in your direction.

When this moment comes – as it will – you can feel well satisfied with your efforts. There is a strong possibility that he will be telling them that he has just had the good fortune to have met a well-respected Senior Citizen who speaks with authority not only on cricket but just about everything.

Then again, he may not.

Another way in which you can quickly establish your credentials as a Senior Citizen is to take a flask of hot water and make your own tea – using the same tea bag every time you repeat the operation. This demonstrates a degree of thrift that will single you out immediately as a Senior Citizen.

It will also help to establish your identity if you have a plastic teaspoon tied to your bag with string.

But if you are feeling more active, the sport for the Senior Citizen is undoubtedly golf.

Golf provides endless opportunities to teach those younger than yourself that recreation is a leisurely pursuit, to be enjoyed to the full and certainly not to be rushed.

A golf course is a beautiful place, and to really enjoy it you don't want to rush round. You have nothing else to do for the rest of the morning or afternoon, so take your time. And don't think for one moment that you are holding up the game behind you. You are not. You are merely slowing them down to your pace so that they, too, can enjoy the delights of the golf course at a leisurely pace.

The delights of a golf course are by no means confined to the fairways. The surrounding woodland is equally interesting and restful, and the opportunity should not be missed to enjoy this to the full by spending as much time as possible in it. This can be easily engineered by hitting every alternate shot into the trees.

The inexperienced younger player may see this as an opportunity to call through any game that may be behind you, and which has probably been held up ever since you left the clubhouse.

But this is, in fact, another opportunity for the Senior Citizen to encourage the game behind to slow down to a more leisurely pace and enjoy the delights of the course as much as you are.

When they come across to the woodland where you are lurking to politely ask what you find so interesting in there, it is an ideal time to share with them your deep knowledge of the flora and fauna, thus enriching their lives considerably.

If by chance, despite your best efforts, you should find yourself actually playing with someone considerably younger, fitter and more able-bodied than yourself, it is not unusual for them to patronise you by making concessions to your age – sorry, maturity. Have none of it. You are more than a match for anyone – both physically and mentally.

As you strike the ball from the first tee and it goes straight as an arrow for a good 25 yards at least, your playing partner will probably ask if you saw where it went. You respond emphatically that of course you did, and set off purposefully in pursuit.

Unfortunately, the chances are that before you reach your ball, you will have forgotten where it went. Don't worry. You'll find it eventually. There will be two balls somewhere up front. Wait for your opponent to head for his, and by a process of elimination, you will find your own!

So when it comes to recreation, the golden rule is never rush – and never be rushed. Slow the action down to your own pace so that everyone around you can benefit from the experience as much as you do.

Here again, it may be useful to have the phone number of the nearest A & E hospital – preferably one with special facilities for removing items of sports equipment from a certain part of one's anatomy.

SHOPPING

Shopping for many people today is not a pleasurable experience. Everything is colourfully packaged, invitingly displayed and competitively priced. But it is all too easy. There's no fun in it any more, either for the shopper or the shopkeeper.

Gone are the days when you could buy two rashers of bacon and a tomato. When the shopkeeper cut his own cheese with a wire, patted his own butter, and sold sugar in a blue paper bag after weighing it out from a sack.

For the majority of Senior Citizens, the supermarket is now the only way to shop. Parking is not a problem – and more importantly, free – it is not too far to walk from vehicle to store and there is usually a welcoming coffee lounge where shell-shocked shoppers can rest after the trauma of being parted from their money.

You can buy everything you want under one roof, from socks to sausages, shaving cream to double cream. You no longer have to visit half a dozen stores to do your weekly shop.

Many would argue that supermarkets have made life easier, quicker and broadened choice. Wrong! The only choice the supermarket shopper makes today is the choice already made for you by the supermarket itself, as any Senior Citizen will tell you at every opportunity.

Gullible shoppers – I exclude Senior Citizens from this category, of course - end up spending pounds more than they intended because they are caressed into the dream world of imaginative selling.

How many shoppers go for two for one offers – buy one get one free? And how many of those wanted even one in the first place? You see them by the dozen checking their bills as they leave the check-outs. 'How did I manage to spend £54.24p when I only came in for bottle of milk and a packet of digestive biscuits?'

Imaginative selling, that's how.

And it's up to the Senior Citizen to redress the balance. To take on the stealthy supermarket merchandising mandarins, and show by example that they can be beaten. That they can be matched move for move by the grey-haired army of cavaliers who refuse to be blinded by the price per kg and take note of the price per pack. Who refuse to be baulked by efforts to confuse the value of everything by sticking resolutely to decimal coinage.

Translate back to real money. That's the only way you can get the true value of anything. A chocolate éclair for 60 pence sounds mere loose change, but when you consider we're talking twelve shillings for a cream cake – puts it all into sharp perspective, doesn't it?

Same with weights and measures. What's a kilogram to someone who's formative years were spent in the local butchers asking for a quarter pound of dripping, or two ounces of boiled ham?

A bottle of milk to a Senior Citizen is a pint. It always has been and it always will be. What's 568 millilitres? It's a pint. Two pints make a quart. Not 1.136 litres. Never has done and never will. Where's the point of that? It's just one more move in the ever-growing tide of confusion that engulfs the masses and gently massages their hard-earned cash out of their pockets and purses and into the tills of the supermarkets.

So how can we as Senior Citizens make our presence felt? Raise the banner for common sense? By maintaining the standards that have served us well for a lifetime, that's how.

As well as the aforementioned tactics of translating decimal coinage back into real money; and new-fangled weights and measures into a language that we all understand, there are a number of ways that the Senior Citizen can set a fine example in the right and wrong way to shop.

But first you have to get yourself noticed, attract attention to yourself to give you as wide an audience as possible when you pass on your little snippets of advice to your fellow shoppers who have not had the benefit of your long experience.

Choice of trolley is important. If you can find one with a wobbly wheel that has a mind of its own when it comes to direction, you are well on your way to getting yourself noticed.

As you run over the foot of some unsuspecting shopper who is unfortunate enough to be in close proximity, you have an excellent opportunity to spread the word. 'You do know those biscuits are nearly two pounds a packet. That's nearly sixpence each. For one <u>biscuit.</u> And they call it a special offer!'

If the person you have spoken to looks blank, it is merely their way of covering up their embarrassment at having this basic fact – which they had hitherto totally overlooked – pointed out to them.

Another way of getting yourself noticed in a supermarket is to do your shopping against the flow of other trolleys. This can cause no end of confusion, quite frequently managing to stop several shoppers at once coming the other way.

For the uninitiated Senior Citizen, this may seem to be counter productive as it would appear to only serve to aggravate other shoppers. Not at all. You will immediately be recognized as a Senior Citizen, the font of all wisdom when it comes to shopping. Any little gems like 'The loose carrots are a better buy than the packaged ones'; and 'don't fall for this organic rubbish' are readily appreciated.

There are many other ways to identify a Senior Citizen, and you would do well to learn a few of them if you have only recently embarked on the long, joy-filled journey to senility.

If you are buying soft fruit, make sure you choose the freshest by pushing your thumb into it to test the quality – you don't buy that particular piece, incidentally. You leave that so that customers who follow you will know you have done the thumb test on their behalf.

Never buy grapes, strawberries, raspberries, gooseberries or any bite-sized soft fruit without first tasting it. Again, your fellow shoppers will thank you or your research work on their behalf.

As you wander from aisle to aisle, taking your time over your selections, translating weights, measures and money back into those of yesteryear, don't stand with your trolley parallel to the aisle, but across it. This effectively reduces the flow of customers considerably.

If you have the good fortune to meet an acquaintance of the Senior Citizen variety, the pair of you, by placing your trolleys at 90 degree angles to the shelves as you exchange pleasantries, can block an aisle completely.

Other ways of manufacturing those magic moments when you are able to strike up a conversation with complete strangers are by pushing off someone else's trolley, seemingly by mistake; and putting a large quantity of items into another person's basket-on-wheels. Both these tactics are guaranteed to attract attention, as the person involved will immediately recognise the actions of a Senior Citizen who is desperate to pass on a piece of intelligence of the utmost importance.

Another useful tactic in the fight to get yourself noticed is to take down most of the stock from a shelf in your search for the item with the longest sell-by date.

If you can engineer a situation where you are into a one-to-one situation with a member of staff, emphasising that things were never like this in your day, that will be a real triumph.

Finally, when you do reach the till, don't use a credit card. That is for young, modern-thinking individuals who know no better. Insist on paying cash. We never bought anything unless we could afford to pay for it.

And even though the till will contain a mountain of cash, insist on giving the right money, or as near as possible, to 'save their change.' For instance, if your shopping bill comes to 4.52p. insist on giving 5.02p, so they can give you a 50 pence piece and 'save their change'.

If you do adopt this practice, work through all the combinations possible, before you actually hand over any money.

I hope, dear Senior Citizen, I have shown you in this section that shopping is far more than an exercise in replenishing food stocks.

It provides many more effective opportunities to educate those less experienced, less fortunate and more gullible than yourself in the ways of the Senior Citizen.

SOPHISTICATION

Sophistication is something that is always evident in the Senior Citizen, but rarely – very rarely – seen in anyone else.

It is to do with genes – you either have it or you don't, and unfortunately it is a fact of genetic life that as mankind's make-up evolves into head-banging disco-manic tendencies, so, sadly, refinement, culture and class are being rapidly eroded.

That is why Senior Citizens are practically the only living genre to have sophistication in abundance – but, worryingly for the rest of mankind, they are not going to be around for ever. So it is of paramount importance that every Senior Citizen recognises his duty to encourage sophistication in every walk of life, otherwise within two decades the word itself will have faded into history.

One doesn't have to be born with a silver spoon clamped firmly between the teeth to exude class. Class, bearing, savoir faire are attainable whatever your station in life. They come from a state of mind, a sure knowledge of what is right (practically everything the Senior Citizen stands for), and what is wrong (what everyone else stands for). A resolute determination to act in a proper manner at all times, regardless of the difficulties and distractions encountered along the way.

Sophistication can be shown in dress, bearing, mannerisms, but probably above all, in taste.

Taste in clothes, cars, food, drink. Brown corduroy trousers for the male, and Harris tweed skirts for the female are typical examples of good taste in clothes. Ripped jeans, grubby tee shirts scrawled with obscene messages are definitely not.

A 1.4 litre 2 door saloon car exudes good taste and sophistication – it is environmentally friendly, value for money, unostentatious and economical to run – exactly the common sense choice one would expect from someone of the maturity and wisdom of the Senior Citizen. Cool, unadulterated sophistication.

Exactly the opposite of the type of vehicle favoured by today's sophistication-starved younger generation – some hideous 4 litre, four wheel drive monster, with blackened windows, high enough off the ground to need a fork lift truck to get behind the wheel and with enough scaffolding welded around the front and rear ends to fend of a herd of rampaging buffalo.

Food and drink are another prime area for demonstrating the true meaning of sophistication and taste. A sit-down meal in a restaurant – even though it may be a two-for-£4.99 early doors offer – is sophistication. A take-away pizza, curry or kebab most definitely is not.

A glass of claret with the meal is sophistication – a lager drunk straight from the bottle most definitely is not.

And so it goes on.

In every walk of life, the Senior Citizen will find an opportunity to demonstrate the true meaning of sophistication, class, taste - a task that is made that much easier by the sloppy, ill-mannered, loutish approach to life demonstrated with monotonous regularity by the younger generation (anyone under the age of 50).

Lead by example. If it means subjecting yourself to the slings and arrows of a few ill-informed louts as you demonstrate your dedication to a bygone age, it is a small price to pay when you consider that you are reinforcing the corner stone on which civilisation was built – and under our influence will continue to flourish for centuries to come.

TRAVEL

HOLIDAYS . . .

We never needed our lives to be organised by any travel agent. There were none of these fancy package holidays to faraway places for us.

Year in, year out we booked the last two weeks in August at Mrs Cartwright's boarding house in Fleetwood. Immediately after the war, when rationing was still on, we had to take our own food, and she prepared it for us.

Later, we went bed and breakfast, and for those who really aspired to life in the fast lane, full board became an option - at a cost, of course. Admittedly, there were certain advantages to full board – usually covered by the words 'fully inclusive'. This usually meant that things like condiments were supplied free of charge, whereas anyone on b & b had to pay a shilling a week extra for 'use of cruet'.

Those lucky enough to eventually move up the holiday pecking order to full board could truly claim to have covered the full gamut of good living.

There were, of course, those who worked practically all their lives without ever reaching the dizzy heights of full board, but that didn't stop them enjoying every precious minute of their annual holiday.

There may have been no such thing as TV in every room, or en suite facilities. We may have had to endure the discomfort of a half hour wait on a draughty landing before relishing the relief of emptying our bladders of a morning, but we certainly knew how to enjoy ourselves.

Today's holidaymakers have missed out on all this. They may be able to fly to Greece or Italy in the time it took us to cover less than 100 miles by road, but are they any better off? Do they return from their fun-in-the-sun breaks refreshed? Not a bit of it. The papers are full of tales of woe from the Costa del Stress. Holidays from hell programmes abound on TV. And why?

Because today's holidaymakers are a commodity to be packaged, transported to their dubious destinations – and charged a fortune for the doubtful privilege.

Holidaymakers think they have never had as wide a choice as they have today. The truth is they have no choice. They go where the holiday packagers want them to go.

Anyone under the age of sensibility - that is everyone who has not yet reached Senior Citizen status - will not realise this.

It is therefore up to every Senior Citizen to lead the fight to once more put the holidaymakers in control of their own destiny, by demonstrating that there is nothing to lose and everything to be gained by demonstrating at every opportunity that only one person should be driving your holiday arrangements - you!

... BY AIR

As you embark on your hard-earned holiday selected by yourself without the hint of interference from any pressure group, the first opportunity you are likely to get to register your status as a Senior Citizen will be when you arrive at the airport by taxi.

If you want to avoid tipping the driver, when you leave the car feign some discomfort because the car was driven too fast (car sickness) or too slow (anxious you would miss your check-in time).

You will have established the cost of the fare before starting the journey, and carefully spread the exact money over some four different pockets. So when you come to pay the fare, you laboriously search each pocket in turn for loose change until you have the right money. By the time you have found enough to pay the fare, the driver will be so anxious to get away, he will tell you to forget the tip.

The next thing you will do is to find yourself a trolley, then put your luggage on it in such a way that it protrudes considerably from each side, thus rattling the shins of anyone unlucky enough to get within striking distance. This will ensure that you have a clear run to the check-in desk, which will invariably be the one with the shortest queue – but the wrong one!

When you reach the front of the queue, which will probably be for a flight to Paris when you are booked on a flight to Palma, you will look totally blank when your mistake is pointed out to you.

This will take some time, as you will have forgotten where you put your tickets and passports. Refuse to understand, refuse to move, until assistance is summoned. You will then be taken to the front of your proper queue, checked in quickly and moved on before you can cause any more disruption.

This is, of course, in the interests of the smooth running of the airport, but it is also invaluable in drawing attention to yourself.

From here on, everyone on your flight will know who you are, and everything you do, everything you stand for will be noticed by your fellow passengers.

If you do feel you still need to draw attention to yourself, when you board the aircraft you can have difficulty finding your seat; hold up the entire boarding process by spending an eternity packing and re-packing your hand baggage into the overhead locker; sitting in the wrong seats; and finally, just before take off, insisting on retrieving some item or other from your hand baggage which will mean that the overhead locker has to be opened again.

If you can engineer it so that the entire contents land on the head of some unsuspecting passenger sat underneath, so much the better. You will then be set for the holiday of a lifetime, where you will be guaranteed at every turn the undivided attention of your fellow holidaymakers.

Go for it – seize the golden opportunity to demonstrate all the values held dear to the Senior Citizen. I can guarantee your efforts will not go unnoticed.

. . . BY LAND

When the Senior Citizen arrives at the hotel – whether it is in this country or overseas – he or she will immediately come across endless opportunities to demonstrate everything they stand for – class, sophistication, style.

You will not accept the first room you are allocated. Every Senior Citizen has a built-in wealth of reasons for wanting a move. The room doesn't have a sea view/does have a sea view/ is too near the disco/ too far away from the disco/too many floors up/ not enough floors up/ too far from the lift/too near the lift – no self-respecting Senior Citizen is ever stuck for a convincing reason to change rooms.

Once you have established your presence among the staff, should you need to reinforce just how important you are, you can continually ring reception/room service for assistance. Can't find the hairdryer/can't use the hairdryer/can't turn the bath taps on/can't turn the bath taps off/ can't get the shower temperature right/can't switch the lights on/ can't switch the lights off.

When you have had a personal visit from the concierge, the housekeeper, the electrician and the chamber maid, you have one more way of establishing beyond all doubt that you are a Senior Citizen. And that is to tell reception you can't find your key.

In most modern hotels, it will be an electronic swipe card. They will give you another one, and you will tell them you can't see how that can possibly work in your door. So they will come up to demonstrate and just as they open the door, you will miraculously find your original key in your handbag/pocket.

After all this, I can guarantee that for the rest of your stay the staff will know who you are and exactly what you stand for.

. . . BY SEA

An increasingly-popular holiday for Senior Citizens is a cruise. It is continuous travel in five star luxury. The downside, however, is that as a Senior Citizen you will have to work particularly hard to get yourself noticed as most of your fellow passengers will also be Senior Citizens.

So to get yourself noticed on a cruise, you will have to behave in such a way that you belie your true age – sorry, degree of maturity..

It won't be easy, but well worth the effort. Because if you are successful, fellow non-Senior Citizen passengers and crew alike will be amazed to find someone who has obviously not yet reached Senior Citizen status behaving in such a responsible manner.

So how do we go about this? Well the golden rule, as always, is look good, feel good.

This will mean regular visits to the hairdressers in the case of ladies, coupled with immediate enrolment into a keep-fit class (not, it must be emphasised, one designed specifically for those of more mature years); while for the men, a healthy tan and shorts will enhance the image. If the legs are beginning to look like something from the antiques road show, a track suit is permissible.

An activity that couples can do together, which will impress onlookers, is to take frequent strolls round the deck in a purposeful manner. This is somewhere between an amble and a power walk. The former will show total lack of purpose and do nothing to underline your fitness; the latter will have you falling by the wayside very smartly, if not worse. You should aim, if you can, to overtake at least one other couple as you walk round the ship. If you find this too difficult, walk round the ship in the opposite direction to everyone else.

All this physical activity may well prove to be totally exhausting – but well worth the effort when you are shown to your table at dinner and seated with other passengers of the Senior Citizen persuasion.

Having gone to great lengths to convince the ship at large during the day of your youthfulness, just watch the faces of your fellow diners when you reveal your real age – but don't forget to add 10 years.

One word of warning. While you may be able to get away with looking physically younger, you must be very wary of allowing those odd senior moments to creep into your lifestyle or conversation.

Whatever you do, at the Captain's cocktail party don't ask whether or not the crew sleep on the ship!

UNDERESTIMATING THE SENIOR CITIZEN

This is probably the biggest mistake a non-Senior Citizen can make.

Any Senior Citizen worthy of the name is superior to lesser mortals in every way – education, intellect, wisdom, skills, experience, sophistication, style. Your general demeanour will of course reflect this, but for those unfortunates who don't immediately get the message, drive it home loud and clear.

If you come up against someone who feels they are superior to you in intellect, match them blow for blow. If they try to get the upper hand by dropping into the conversation that they went to Oxford, you counter with your time in Cambridge.

You don't have to go into detail, particularly if your only experience of Cambridge was a weekend break on a caravan site. Just establishing the fact you were there will give you the upper hand.

If they try to dazzle you with their superior sporting prowess, outdo them. Remember, you will find this easier if you claim international honours in something fairly obscure, like canal-jumping or leap frog. But make absolutely sure from the outset that your adversary knows nothing at all about the sport, otherwise you will have handed him the trump card to wipe out your ace.

And if it comes down to the physical, calmly point out your record as the East Midlands light middleweight army boxing champion in 1955. If this fails to impress and your tormentor is built like a steam hammer and things are looking decidedly uncomfortable for you, this could be the ideal moment to mention your frozen shoulder, in-growing toe nail or any other infirmity that will prevent you embarking on any stressful physical activity.

This isn't cowardice, but one more area in which you will be showing your superiority as a Senior Citizen by using your wits and guile to get yourself out of what was looking like developing into a decidedly sticky situation.

USELESS INFORMATION

Again, something that is the prerogative of everyone else – never Senior Citizens.

They are always well-informed, an authority on every subject under the sun, and ready to share their vast knowledge and experience of life with anyone, with little or no encouragement. The more obscure the information you are sharing, the more you are likely to get away with it, as the person with whom you are sharing it won't have a clue what you are talking about.

They will, however, go away full of admiration.

'How thoughtful of that Senior Citizen to share his knowledge of the life cycle of the water vole,' they will think as they leave the train after a two-hour journey.

'How fortunate we found a seat next to someone like that. If we hadn't been so lucky, we would have had to spend the entire journey reading that book we've been trying to finish for weeks.'

You can also help to relieve pressure on the National Health Service by sharing your wide knowledge of medicine with whoever you are seated next to in the doctor's waiting room.

It goes without saying, of course, that the only people in a doctor's waiting room who are genuinely ill are Senior

Citizens. Everyone in there of working age is a malingerer and a shirker.

So do your bit to take the pressure off the NHS by strategically seating yourself next to a non-Senior Citizen and finding out what they have come to see the doctor about.

Armed with this information you can regale them with stories of all your relatives, friends and acquaintances who have experienced something similar, and the fact that not one of them found any cure in a doctor's surgery. In fact in a number of cases, the condition proved fatal.

In all probability, you will find that the person to whom you have been talking will suddenly feel better and leave, thus reducing the number waiting to see the doctor by one. You then strike up a conversation with someone else, and follow the same procedure. This tactic will not only relieve pressure on the NHS by reducing the number of patients, but will dramatically shorten your own waiting time.

And should you be unfortunate enough to try this tactic on anyone who is genuinely suffering from something extremely painful in an embarrassing part of his anatomy, and who not only threatens to stick his steel-capped boot in your nether regions but is actually driven to carry out his threat by what he considers to be your aimless, meaningless rambling, you couldn't be in a better place to receive immediate treatment.

VALUE FOR MONEY

There are many savings to be made by the Senior Citizen by discriminate shopping. Apart from the obvious – two for one offers, bargain counters for items approaching their sell by date – there can often be bargains to be had from the bread, cakes and sandwiches counter just before closing time.

If there aren't any special offers, ask. Put in a bid. Anything perishable left unsold at the end of the day will probably only end up in a skip. By taking it off their hands, you will not only be treating yourself to a good buy, but doing them a favour by reducing their costs for waste disposal.

You may find that some stores will tell you that their unsold food at the end of the day goes to the poor and needy. Point out that they need look no further.

I'm not suggesting for one minute you give the impression that you are seeking 'bargains' for yourself, but for a very good friend/aging relative. No self-respecting Senior Citizen will ever admit to being financially unsound, or indeed unsound in any other department.

Before you leave the supermarket you may fancy some light refreshment after all that hard bargaining.

Here again, the prudent Senior Citizen can make a considerable saving by being observant. Keep an eye open for a young mother with at least one child in need of undivided attention.

Chances are that mum will have bought some kind of refreshment for the children, as well as something for herself. If your luck is in, she will have had neither the time nor the inclination to enjoy her own snack, and will leave it untouched. A quick sleight of hand – this can be acquired by practice at home - will deftly transfer said pastry to your tray before it can be cleared away by the staff.

Another saving, another triumph!

Another way to keep the Senior Citizen away from the official ranks of the poor and needy, thus saving the Government cash in the long run in supplementary benefits and giving another example to those with lesser experience of life than yourself of how ingenuity brings its own rewards.

VALUES

Wherever you are, whatever you are doing, whatever company you are in – and particularly when in the company of anyone younger than yourself, which will be just about everyone - you must impress on them a sense of values, which, of course, only the Senior Citizen has.

At every conceivable opportunity, utter one of the following phrases loud and clear so that everyone within earshot gets the message:

It's not what you've got, it's what you do with it.

It's not what you pay for something, its what value you put on it.

And it's not a matter of what you can take out of society, but what you can put into it.

There is no guarantee of course that your well-chosen words of wisdom will be appreciated by all, but it will probably ensure for you a rapid promotion to the top of the waiting list for an all-expenses paid holiday in a psychiatric ward.

VIEWING HABITS

Watching TV is something Senior Citizens rarely admit to doing. They prefer to spend their time in more worthwhile and rewarding ways.

They socialise a great deal, become involved in pastimes that demand a lot of concentration and brain power, research their family tree, attend information technology classes, or are members of a book reading circle.

On the evenings they don't go out or entertain - because Senior Citizens are in great demand as dinner guests and therefore are frequently finding themselves in a position where they have to return the invitations – they tend to read a lot.

A typical Senior Citizen would buy one of the serious broadsheets on a Sunday and make it last all week (this is also a fine demonstration of the Senior Citizen's sense of value for money). So when it comes to viewing habits, Senior Citizens don't have much time to establish any.

But there are times when TV cannot be avoided, and a choice has to be made. Senior Citizens will admit to watching only BBC2 – occasionally BBC 1 for the news programmes and Panorama.

Many Senior Citizens may possess a free-to-view digibox, which gives them many more programmes without any additional cost once they have acquired the box.

But they will never admit to owning one. If they were to do so, it would acknowledge two things: that they are sufficiently interested in television to want a wider variety of programmes, indicating that they spend far too much time watching it; and that they are not in the financial league of those who subscribe to satellite TV.

One of the problems of Senior Citizenship is that the Senior Citizen brain is packed so tightly with memories, wisdom and experience that eventually some things are inevitably consigned to the waste bin. They have to be. This is not the same as loss of memory – short term or otherwise. It is simply because the human brain can only store so much information, and when it is full, some of it has to be cast aside.

I mention this at this point because many folk who do not appreciate the finer points of Senior Citizenship may get the impression that when the Senior Citizen doesn't readily join in any conversation about what was on TV last night, it is because they can't remember.

Not a bit of it. It is simply that, to the Senior Citizen, what was on TV last night would be totally irrelevant, and therefore would be consigned immediately to that waste bin to preserve more space in the brain for matters of more importance.

So what is the point in watching it in the first place?

WINE

There is more snobbery surrounding the drinking of wine than any other subject. This doesn't apply to the Senior Citizen of course. The Senior Citizen knows what he or she likes, regardless of price or year, and no fancy talk will convince them otherwise.

There are basically three acceptable occasions on which you may drink wine – at home when you are having a quiet night in; at home when you are entertaining; or in a restaurant.

Choice of wine for a quiet night in is a doddle. Go to the local supermarket, pay a modest price for a very palatable and reasonable wine. You won't go far wrong. Wines, spirits and beers contribute a great deal to supermarket profits. They are in keen competition, so cannot afford to leave anything to chance.

They employ the best wine buyers to give their customers the best value for money – even for the most discerning palate. As a general rule, you will get excellent value for money in a supermarket. The more you pay, the better the wine. Chances are that unless you are a real aficionado, you will get a perfectly acceptable bottle for £3.99.

Choice of wine in a restaurant may take a little more care if you are not to be palmed off with something very average at a cost that you will need a second mortgage to cover.

When you are presented with the wine list, chances are that it will resemble something the size of a modest telephone directory, and unless you are a true buff, much of it will be totally meaningless.

The way to impress in a restaurant is to study the wine list at length, then ask for the house wine, with the comment that a good restaurant would never contemplate serving a poor house wine. This will bring you a perfectly palatable wine without breaking the bank .

The third scenario needs a bit more ingenuity – entertaining to impress at home.

Trust your judgement. Choose a modestly-priced wine from the supermarket that you are happy with. Choose a meat dish, so that you can serve a red wine, and pour it into a decanter before serving. This way, your guests will not see the label.

Strategically place an impressive-looking guide book to the best wines in the world somewhere you can easily draw attention to it while you are having a pre-dinner drink, and talk with some authority on a couple of examples you happen to have memorised.

When you do go in for dinner, point out that the wine you are serving is better for being decanted, pick up your glass, savour the bouquet, then slowly taste the wine. Don't sip – take a meaningful mouthful, and make no secret of your rapture at such a memorable experience. Then ask for your guests' opinion. I can guarantee that unless you're unlucky enough to have unwittingly invited one of the world's expert wine tasters, you will get nothing but praise.

If you really want to impress, keep your eye on the local bottle bank. If you come across an impressive looking label, take the bottle home, remove the label and slap it on a bottle of cheap plonk before putting it on the table.

With a bit of care, you can make that label last for anything up to a dozen times.

WORK ETHIC

If there is one thing as certain as the fact that night follows day, it is that young people today do not know the meaning of the word work. Mention a fair day's work for a fair day's pay, and they will look at you as if you come from another planet.

We worked all the hours that God sent in order to scrape together a meagre pittance on which we not only had to exist, but provide a roof over our heads, a decent standard of living and the odd treat besides for the very generation that now look on our efforts with scorn.

They don't know they're born today, compared to what we had to put up with, and it's up to us to put them right at every opportunity.

Whenever you hear mention of how hard done by they are because they have to work a 35 hour week, point out that we used to work a 35-hour day. If the nit-pickers insist on pointing out that there aren't 35 hours in a day, you tell them that we did the equivalent of 35 hours in a day.

Whenever you hear mention of five or six weeks holiday a year, point out that we had to work for 30 years before we got a holiday at all, then it was just a week if you were lucky.

And you couldn't take it when it suited. You had to take it when you were told.

And whenever you hear mention of folk going to Barbados for the winter, or Tenerife for a couple of months, point out that the only reason we had for taking more than a week off work was death.

And what's all this health and safety in the workplace about? There were no fancy rules and regulations to protect the workers in our day. It was every man for himself.

If a brick dropped on you on a building site and fractured your skull, they wanted to know what you were doing sticking your head in the way. And you'd probably get a bill for the brick if it broke!

Survival of the fittest – that was the only rule we worked to. And if you weren't fit, you didn't survive. End of story.

When we talked about working to rule in our day, there was only one set of rules you worked to – those dictated by the boss. If you didn't like it, you knew what you could do.

As for workers rights, the only rights we had were the right to work our socks off. And if you didn't, the management exercised their rights – to pack you off down the road quicker than a rat up a drainpipe.

But we were happy.

How many of these young folk on £100,000 a year with three months holiday a year and every winter in Mauritius can say that?

X RAYS (including hospitals, illness)

X rays are something you went to hospital for when you were genuinely ill.

And that's another thing that the younger generation know nothing about today.

Most of them spend more time in hospital than they do at work. They have these private health plans that cover them for every mortal thing – from having their toe nails cut to blowing their noses. When they're not actually In hospital, they're complaining about the length of hospital waiting lists.

And they've got the bare-faced check to blame the Senior Citizen for causing the NHS to seize up, such are the demands they are putting on the medical services.

What utter nonsense. That is not in the Senior Citizen's nature. When a Senior Citizen is ill, the last thing he or she will do is go running to the doctor, or book themselves in to one of these fancy £1000 a day clinics while they have a nervous breakdown, small bits enlarged, large bits reduced or flabby bits moved about to give them more shape.

Senior Citizens of today can boast, quite rightly, that they were very rarely ill. The life they lived made them tough, able to stand up to anything that nature threw at them. And so busy were they earning a living, looking after their families and attending to all those little jobs that make a home run smoothly that they didn't have time to be ill.

This doesn't apply to everyone, of course. Some folk of our generation were genuinely ill. Some were seriously ill and had to go into hospital. Some, sadly, never came out.

But for the majority of Senior Citizens, there was rarely anything wrong that couldn't be put right with a good old fashioned remedy, the secrets of which had been passed down from generation to generation.

Which self-respecting Senior Citizen today cannot recall rubbing a dock leaf on a sting to take the pain away?

How many Senior Citizens would have been a martyr to chest complaints if it hadn't been for goose grease, bread poultices or comfrey?

And who would have dreamed of rushing off to the health centre – if we'd had such a thing in our day – with a sprained wrist, to have it bound up and be given a sick note for a fortnight?

So, Senior Citizens, if you wish to do your bit to relieve the pressure on hospital waiting lists, spread the word about this wealth of home remedies learned at your mother's knee and do your utmost to get them universally adopted once again.

We may not live as long as the youngsters of today, but at least we'll die free of all additives and preservatives.

YOUNG PEOPLE

I have referred repeatedly throughout this reference book to 'young people'.

Perhaps this is a good time to define the species.

Young people are any human beings of a lesser age than ourselves – which probably includes about 95 per cent of the population. But above all, they are people of any age who do not have the foresight to see that everything the Senior Citizen stands for is right, while everything that they stand for is totally wrong.

It is an uphill struggle, granted, but if each of us can strive to change just one aspect of a young person's behaviour pattern in accordance with the gospel according to the Senior Citizen, their lives will be greatly enriched.

The battle will not be won, but mankind will be well on the way to regaining the sanity that is fast disappearing in the misguided name of progress.

ZERO TOLERANCE

The Senior Citizen has zero tolerance of anyone who disagrees with him or her. As we get older, this number will increase, but we should never weaken.

Senior Citizens the world over must stand shoulder to shoulder to stem the tide of ignorance and prejudice that is threatening to engulf society.

There is only one way forward if civilisation as we have known it is to survive.

Our way.

Not only do we have a right to be heard, but a duty to make ourselves heard.

Remember always the battle cry of the Senior Citizen – stand up, speak up – but never shut up!